영문독해의
Bible

영어 순해

Basic

영어순해 BASIC

지은이 김영로
펴낸이 임상진
펴낸곳 (주)넥서스

초판 1쇄 발행 2000년 4월 20일

2판 1쇄 발행 2005년 4월 5일
2판 12쇄 발행 2010년 9월 10일

3판 1쇄 발행 2011년 1월 25일
3판 20쇄 발행 2024년 8월 5일

출판신고 1992년 4월 3일 제311-2002-2호
주소 10880 경기도 파주시 지목로 5
전화 (02)330-5500 팩스 (02)330-5555
ISBN 978-89-5797-466-7 13740

www.nexusbook.com

영문독해의
Bible

영문독해의 기본 원리

영어 순해

김영로 지음

Basic

넥서스

머리말

영문장 이해의 가장 큰 잘못!

영어를 배우는 우리나라 사람들은 물론, 우리들의 영어 선생님들과 영어교재 저자들까지도 저지르는 가장 흔한 잘못이 있다.

> **보기1** A goal worked toward half-heartedly is seldom achieved.
>
> 마지못해 세워진 목적은 거의 성취되지 못한다. (어느 책의 번역)

이 번역문을 보고 아무 잘못도 발견하지 못하는 사람은 분명히 영어를 잘못 공부해온 사람이다. 왜냐하면 얼핏 보아 이 번역문에는 아무런 잘못이 없어 보이지만, 영어를 모국어로 하는 사람(the native speaker of English)처럼 영어 원문을 순서대로 따져보면 다음과 같은 뜻이 나타나기 때문이다.

> 목표는 / (만일 그 목표를) 향해 열성이 없이 일(=노력)하면 / 거의 성취되지 않는다.
> → 목표는 / 그것을 성취하기 위해 열심히 노력하지 않으면 / 거의 성취되지 않는다.

영어 원문을 다음과 같이 바꾸어보면 그 의미가 더욱 분명해진다.

> → A goal that is worked toward half-heartedly is seldom achieved.
> = A goal, if it is worked toward half-heartedly, is seldom achieved.
> = If you work toward your goal half-heartedly, you seldom achieve it.

> **보기2** Instead of being dumped into a nearby river or lake, sewage is sent to a giant tank where the water is purified.
>
> 하수오물은 강이나 호수 근처에 버려지는 것이 아니라 물이 정화되는 큰 탱크로 보내진다. (어느 책의 번역)

보기 1에서는 worked toward half-heartedly가 앞에 나온 명사 goal을 수식하는 말이라는 이유로 이 부분을 먼저 번역해서 '목적' 앞에 붙이려고 했기 때문에 어처구니없는 잘못이 저질러졌다. 보기 2에서도 where 이하가 tank를 수식하는 말이라는 이유로 이것을 먼저 보고 옮겨서 위로 붙이려고 함으로써 마찬가지로 어처구니없는 오류를 범했다. 이런 실수는 다음과 같이 앞에서 순서대로 살펴보았더라면 충분히 피할 수 있었을 것이다.

인근 강이나 호수에 버려지지 않고, 하수는 거대한 탱크로 보내져서, <u>거기서 정화된다.</u>

이렇게 영어의 본래 순서를 따라 내려오면서 살폈더라면 the water는 단순히 '물'이 아니라 sewage를 가리킨다는 것을 알아챘을 것이다.

독해 및 번역 능력은 물론 작문 능력도 향상된다

차례를 보면 알 수 있듯이, 이 책은 우리나라 사람들이 영어를 배우는 데에 필요한 여러 가지 중요한 정보를 제공해 준다.

이 책을 처음부터 끝까지 철저히 소화하고 나면 원어민처럼 영어를 순서대로 읽어나가면서 바로 내용을 이해할 수 있게 될 뿐만 아니라, 전통적인 방법으로 접근하는 사람들보다 훨씬 더 빠르게 영어를 우리말로 옮길 수 있게 될 것이다. 한 걸음 더 나아가서 작문을 염두에 두고 이 책을 보고 나면 영어로 글을 쓰는 데에 자신감도 얻게 될 것이다.

김영로

〈김영로 선생의 순해 시리즈〉
· 『영어순해 BASIC』 - 영어 문장의 서술 방식을 이해하고, 문장의 전개 순서대로 뜻을 파악하는 법을 익힌다.
· 『영어순해』 - 직독직해 원리를 터득하여 영문독해 능력을 향상시킨다.
· 『문맥순해』 - 문장을 전부 다 읽지 않고도 순식간에 뜻을 파악하는, 빠른 독해를 위한 비결을 전해 받는다.

차 례

|일러두기| 표기 부호 설명

A : B	B는 A와 같은 뜻의 표현이다.
A = B	A와 B는 사전적으로는 같은 뜻은 아니지만, 문맥상 같은 의미로 쓰인 것으로서, 그 문장 안에서 A대신 B를 사용할 수 있다.
note A = B	B는 A와 같은 뜻의 표현으로서, A대신 문장에서 사용할 수 있다.
A 〈 B	B는 A의 기본이 되는 표현이다. 즉 A는 B에서 파생된 표현이다.

part 1

영어의 서술 순서

이봐! 이봐!
순서대로 해야
뜻이 풀리지~!

4. 8. 3.
1. 5. 7 …

1. 서론

모국어를 듣거나 읽을 때에 순서대로 따라가지 않고, '거꾸로' — 다시 말해서, 뒤에서 앞으로 거슬러 올라오면서 — 듣거나 읽는 사람은 없다. 이것은 외국어의 경우에도 마찬가지이다. 어떤 외국어를 제대로 하는 사람은, 그것을 모국어로 사용하는 사람들같이, 그것을 차례대로 듣거나 읽어 나가면서 동시에 이해한다. 그러므로 우리가 영어를 배울 때에 처음부터 이런 습관을 길러야 한다고 필자는 믿는다. 이런 습관을 기르기 위해, 영어 문장이 어떤 순서와 형태로 전개되고 표현되는지 살펴보자.

① He tried again / only to fail.
　　　제1동작　　　　　　제2동작 (부정사구)

이 문장은 다음 발전과정을 거쳐 형성된 것으로 볼 수 있다.

(a) He tried again. He only failed. (두 개의 독립 문장)
(b) He tried again **but** he only failed. (한 개의 중문)
→ He tried again only to fail. (하나의 단문)
　　그는 다시 시도했으나 / 실패했을 뿐이었다.

예문 1에서는 제2동작을 'to'-infinitive로 표현하고 있는데, 이것이 한국어와 다른 점이다. 그리고 to fail의 실제 시제는 주절의 정동사 tried와 같이 '과거'이다.

② The train leaves here at ten a.m., / arriving there at two p.m.
　　　　　　제1동작　　　　　　　　　　　　　제2동작 (부정사구)

= (a) The train leaves here at ten a.m. It arrives there at two p.m. (두 문장)
= (b) The train leaves here at ten a.m. **and** (it) arrives there at two p.m. (중문)
→ The train leaves here at ten a.m., arriving there at two p.m. (단문)
　　그/이 기차는 여기를 오전 10시에 떠나서, / 거기에 오후 2시에 도착한다.

예문 2에서는 제 2동작을 현재분사로 표현하고 있으며, arriving의 실제 시제는 정동사 leaves와 같이 현재이다.

3
He failed again / to our disappointment.
제1동작   제2동작 (전치사구)

= (a) He failed again. We were disappointed. (두 문장)
= (b) He failed again, **and** we were disappointed. (중문)
= (c) He failed again, **so** (that) we were disappointed. (중문 또는 복문)

그가 또 다시 실패해서 / 우리는 실망했다.

여기서는 제2동작이 '전치사구' 안에 명사로 표현되어 있다.

관찰

영어에서는 두 개의 동작이 차례로 발생하는 경우에, 일반적으로

1) 첫째 동작은 '정동사' (the finite verb = 술어동사) 형태로 제시하고,
2) 둘째 동작은 부정사나 분사로, 또는 전치사구 안에 명사로 나타낸다.

Faith will move mountains.

2. 부정사구

1 They parted / never to see each other again.

    = (a) They parted. They never saw each other again.
    = (b) They parted **and** (they) never saw each other again.
        그들은 헤어지고 나서 / 한 번도 서로를 다시 만나지 못했다.

    부정사의 이런 용법은 다음 예문에 잘 나타나 있다.

    (a) He came **and** saw me last week. [informal English]
    (b) He came to see me last week. [standard written English]

    구조적으로 (b)는 (a)보다 더 발전된 형태라고 볼 수 있다.

2 Two atoms of hydrogen combine with one atom of oxygen / to form water.

    = Two atoms of hydrogen combine with one atom of oxygen **and** form water.
    두 원자의 수소가 한 원자의 산소와 결합해서 / 물을 형성한다.

    `note` combine 결합하다 | form (v.): make 만들다

3 You should exercise regularly / to stay fit. [단문]

    = You should exercise regularly **if** you are to stay fit. [복문]

다음 두 번역을 비교해 보라.

(A) 건강을 유지하려면 / 우리는 규칙적으로 운동해야 한다. (재래식)
(B) 우리는 규칙적으로 운동해야 / 건강을 유지할 수 있다. (김영로식)

영어의 어순을 그대로 따라가면서 이해하는 버릇을 기르기 위해 필자는 (B)가 바람직한 방식이라고 생각한다.

📖 문법

(a) You should exercise regularly to stay fit. (informal English)
(b) One should exercise regularly to stay fit. (standard written English)

여기서 You나 One은 '상대방' 이나 '어떤 한 사람' 이 아니라 '일반적인 사람' 을 가리킨다.

note stay fit: to stay in shape: stay healthy (건강한 상태에 머무르다 →) 건강을 유지하다

---

4 Action / to be effective / must be directed to clearly conceived ends.

= (a) Action, if it is to be effective, must be directed to clearly conceived ends.
= (b) If it is to be effective, action must be directed to clearly conceived ends.
= (c) Action must be directed to clearly conceived ends if it is to be effective.
= (d) To be effective, action must be directed to clearly conceived ends.
= (e) Action must be directed to clearly conceived ends to be effective.

행동은 / 소기의 결과를 가져오려면 / 분명하게 생각해낸 목적을 향해 기울여져야 한다.

note effective: producing a desired result 바라는 결과를 가져오는 | direct one's attention or efforts to / toward ~을 위해 주의·노력 따위를 기울이다 | conceive: to form or develop in the mind 생각해내다 | end (n.): a purpose 목적

5 When a new style in clothes appears, women usually hasten to conform.

새로운 스타일이 의상에 나타나면, 여성들은 대개 서둘러 따른다.

note hasten to do = to be quick to do: quickly do 서둘러 하다 | conform (to) ~에 따르다

6 Whenever he passes a mirror, he stops to pat his hair into place.

= Whenever he passes a mirror, he stops and pats his hair into place.

그는 거울을 지나갈 때마다, 발걸음을 멈추고 머리를 다독거려 제자리에 들여보낸다.

연구

(a) put ~ into place 제자리에 집어넣다 (기본 표현)
(b) pat ~ into place 다독거려 제자리에 집어넣다 (파생 표현)

순해

다음 표현들은 이런 식으로 정리하라.

take the trouble to do 수고해서 하다 → 수고럽게 하다
take pains to do 애를 써서 하다
take the initiative to do 앞장서서 하다
lower oneself to do 자신을 낮추어서 하다 → 비열하게 하다
bring oneself to do 자신을 데리고 가서 하다 → 자신에게 강요해서 하다

EXERCISE
순해순역 연습

1. (a) You must be 21 / to drink in Arizona.

   (b) You really have to live there / to know that country.

   (c) In this field, one must study for many years / to become an expert.

   (d) You have only to read a few pages / to find that this book is really good.

   (e) One doesn't need to be a cook / to criticize the cooking.

   (f) A man / to carry on a successful business / must have imagination.

🖐 **표현**

have to do 해야 한다
have only to do 하기만 하면 된다
do not have to do 하지 않아도 된다

📖 **연구**

1. (a) carry on a successful business 〔형용사를 이용한 표현 형태〕
 = (b) carry on business successfully 〔부사를 이용한 표현 형태〕

2. (a) They had a hasty lunch.
 = (b) They had lunch in haste. 그들은 허겁지겁 점심 식사를 했다.

2. (a) It takes about 80 calories of heat / to melt one gram of ice.

 (b) It takes many years of training / to become an expert in this field.

 = One must train for many years to become an expert in this field.

note melt 녹이다 | expert 전문가 | train (v.) 훈련을 받다

3. (a) The salmon fights its way back up the river / to lay its eggs.

 (b) Salmons spend most of their adult lives in salt water, though they return to their freshwater birthplaces / to spawn and die.

문법

(a) A fox is a wild animal. 〔일반적인 문어체 영어〕
(b) The fox is a wild animal. 〔딱딱한 문어체 영어〕
(c) Foxes are wild animals. 〔구어체 영어〕

표현

다음 표현들은 이런 식으로 정리하라.

(a) make one's way 가다 〔기본 표현〕
(b) walk one's way 걸어서 가다 〔파생 표현〕
(c) shoot one's way 총을 쏘면서 가다
(d) fight one's way (여러 가지 어려움과) 싸우면서 가다
(e) work one's way 일을 하면서 가다
(f) think one's way 생각을 통해서 가다
(g) read one's way 독서를 통해서 가다
(h) bribe one's way 뇌물을 주고 가다
(i) worm one's way 벌레처럼 기어서 가다
(j) inch one's way 천천히 가다

4. (a) Come by / to pick me up at your convenience.

    (b) My grandparents emigrated from Spain / to come to the United States.

 구문

(a) at your convenience (부사구)
= when it is convenient for you (부사절)

5. Green plants use sunlight / to convert carbon dioxide and water into sugar and oxygen.

note convert: to change 바꾸다 | carbon dioxide 이산화탄소 | oxygen 산소

6. Psycholinguistics brings together the theoretical and empirical resources of both psychology and linguistics / to examine the mental processes underlying the use of language.

note psycholinguistics 언어심리학 | bring together = combine; use 결합하다; 사용하다 | theoretical 이론적인
〈 theory 이론 | empirical 경험적인 〈 experience 경험 | resource = data; knowledge 자료; 지식 |
examine = to study 연구하다 | mental process (마음의 과정 →) 두뇌의 사고 또는 인지 기능 | underlie ~의 밑에
놓여 있다; ~의 기초가 되다

 구문

underlying the use of language (분사구)
= that underlie the use of language (관계사절)

다음 두 번역 중 어느 것이 합리적인지 생각해 보라.

(A) 언어심리학은 / 언어 사용의 기초가 되는 정신적 작용을 조사하는 / 심리학과 언어학 모두에 관한 이론적이며 경험적인 자료들을 수집한다.

(B) 언어심리학은 심리학과 언어학 양쪽의 이론적, 경험적 지식을 이용하여 / 언어 사용의 기초가 되는 두뇌의 사고 또는 인지 기능을 연구한다.

이 문장은 다음과 같이 바꾸어 쓸 수 있다.

(a) Psycholinguistics uses the theoretical and empirical resources of both psychology and linguistics to examine the mental processes underlying the use of language.

(b) Psycholinguistics, using the theoretical and empirical resources of both psychology and linguistics, examines the mental processes underlying the use of language.

7. One morning a man came out of his house / to find the trunk of his car pushed in. He was relieved to see a note under the windshield. Then he read it: "As I am writing this, fifty people are watching me. They think I am giving you my name, address, license number and insurance company. I'm not!"

note pushed in 밀려서 안으로 들어가 있는 | relieve 안심하게 만들다 | windshield (바람방패 →) 자동차 앞부분의 유리창 | license 면허증 | insurance 보험 | company 회사

8. The Western tourist arrives in China / with the intention of indulging in some frantic China-watching — only to find / that one of the national pastimes of the natives is watching him.

tourist 관광객 | intention 의도 | indulge in ~에 빠지다 | frantic: passionate 열렬한 | pastime 즐겁게 시간을 보내기 위해 하는 일; 오락; 취미 〈 **pass time** 시간을 보내다 | natives 원주민들 = Chinese 중국인들

표현

indulge in China-watching (= do frantic China-watching)
= watch China **frantically** 중국을 열심히 관찰하다

주어진 문장은 다음과 같이 바꾸어 쓸 수 있다.

The Western tourist arrives in China to do some frantic China-watching — only to find that the Chinese also watch him as frantically.

서구의 관광객이 중국에 와서 열심히 중국을 좀 관찰하려고 하는데 — 알고 보니 중국인들 역시 마찬가지로 열심히 자기를 관찰한다.

---

9. Each year thousands of books are published, many of them to attract momentary attention / only to disappear gradually from the shelves and the minds of readers — a few to remain in circulation / as long as books are read.

---

publish 발행하다 | attract: to draw 끌다 | momentary: temporary; brief 일시적인; 잠시 동안의 | attention 주의 | gradually 점차 | shelf 선반; 서가 | circulation 유통 | as long as ~하는 한

순해

"remain / in circulation"에 대한 접근

(A) 유통 속에 남아 있다 [재래식]
(B) 남아서 / 유통되다 [김영로식]

3. '후속' 분사구

① A typhoon struck the city, leaving thousands of people homeless.

= (a) A typhoon struck the city. It left thousands of people homeless.
= (b) A typhoon struck the city **and** it left thousands of people homeless.
= (c) A typhoon struck the city, and as a result thousands of people lost their homes.

태풍이 그 도시를 강타해서, 수천 명의 사람들이 집을 잃었다.

② It is not thought proper for people to gather in groups, blocking the way.

다음 두 번역 중 어느 것이 합리적인지 생각해 보라.
(A) 통행을 막으며, 떼를 지어 사람들이 모이는 것은 바르다고 생각되지 않는다.
(B) 사람들이 모여서 떼를 지어, **길을 막는 것은** 올바른 일로 생각되지 않는다.

'모이는' 동작이 '길을 막는' 동작에 선행하므로 필자는 **(B)**가 합리적이라고 생각한다. **(A)**는 재래식 번역이고, **(B)**는 필자의 새로운 시도이다.

순해

"gather / in groups"

(A) 떼를 지어 모이다 [재래식]
(B) 모여서 / 떼를 이루다 (= gather and form groups) [김영로식]

❸ He greeted her politely, offering her coffee, which she declined.

= (a) He greeted her politely. He offered her coffee. She declined it.
= (b) He greeted her politely **and** offered her coffee, **but** she declined it.
= (c) Greeting her politely, he offered her coffee, which she declined.

그는 그녀에게 공손히 인사하고, 그녀에게 커피를 권했으나, 그것을 그녀는 거절했다.

❹ The burning of coal is a process of chemical change / in which oxygen in the air unites with carbon from the coal, giving off light and heat.

= (a) The burning of coal is a process of chemical change. In this process oxygen in the air unites with carbon from the coal, giving off light and heat.
= (b) The burning of coal is a process of chemical change in which oxygen in the air unites with carbon from the coal **and** gives off light and heat.

석탄의 연소는 화학적 변화의 과정인데, 여기에서는 공기 중의 산소가 석탄에서 나오는 탄소와 결합해서, 빛과 열을 내뿜는다.

note **unite = to combine** 결합하다 ㅣ **give off: to emit** 내뿜다; 방출하다

Everything is possible for the person who has faith.

- Mark 9:23

---

4. 관계사절과 단축 관계사절

❶ We all said prayers / that were never answered.

다음 두 번역 가운데 어느 것이 합리적인지 생각해 보라.

(A) 우리는 모두 / 한 번도 이루어지지 않는 / 기도를 했다. 〔재래식〕

(B) 우리는 모두 기도를 했으나, / 그 기도는 한 번도 이루어지지 않았다. 〔김영로식〕

'기도한' 행위가 '이루어지는 것'에 선행하므로 (A)는 불합리하다.

= (a) We all said prayers. They were never answered.

= (b) We all said prayers, **but** they were never answered.

❷ A man can succeed at anything / for which he has unlimited enthusiasm.

다음 세 번역 가운데 어느 것이 합리적인지 생각해 보라.

(A) 사람은 / 거기에 대해서 무한한 열성을 갖고 있는 / 어떤 일에서든지 성공할 수 있다. 〔재래식 1〕

(B) 사람은 / 무한한 열성을 갖고 있는 / 어떤 일에서든지 성공할 수 있다. 〔재래식 2〕

(C) 사람은 어떤 일에서든지 성공할 수 있다, 거기에 대해서 무한한 열성을 갖고 있다면 말이다. 〔김영로식〕

(A)와 (B)에서는 '열성을 갖고 있는' 주체가 마치 '어떤 일'이라는 그릇된 인상을 주며, 또한 (A)에서는 '거기'가 무엇을 가리키는지 분명하지 않다. 특히 (A)는 '올려번역'이 가져오는 번역문의 어색함을 웅변적으로 잘 보여준다.

주어진 문장은 다음과 같이 바꾸어 쓸 수 있다.

A man can succeed at anything **if** he has unlimited enthusiasm for it.

3 (a) Shoes / that are too tight / deform the feet.
(b) Joys / divided / are increased. (단축 관계사절)

(a) If shoes are too tight, they deform the feet.
 = If they are too tight, shoes deform the feet.
 = Shoes deform the feet if they are too tight.
 = Shoes, if they are too tight, deform the feet.
　　구두는 / 너무 꼭 끼면 / 발의 모양을 찌그러뜨린다.

(b) Joys / that are divided / are increased.
 = Joys, if they are divided, are increased.
 = Joys are increased if they are divided.
 = If they are divided, joys are increased.
　　기쁨은 / 나누면 / 커진다.

Mature love is union under the condition
of preserving one's integrity, one's individuality.

- Erich Fromm

EXERCISE
순해순역 연습

1. Last September, Rangoon university students staged a demonstration / that turned into a riot.

다음 두 번역 중 어느 것이 합리적인지 생각해 보라.

(A) 지난 9월, 랭군의 대학생들이 / 폭동으로 바뀐 / 시위를 벌였다.

(B) 지난 9월, 랭군의 대학생들이 시위를 벌였는데, / 그 시위는 폭동으로 바뀌었다.

2. On his wedding day Jack was in a car accident / that landed him in the hospital for three weeks.

다음 두 번역 중 어느 것이 합리적인지 생각해 보라.

(A) 그의 결혼식 날에 잭은 / 3주일 동안 입원하게 만든 / 자동차 사고를 당했다.

(B) 자기 결혼식 날에 잭은 자동차 사고를 당해서 / 병원에서 3주일 동안 지내게 되었다.

3. He was an enormously wealthy man. But he had a quiet, unassuming way about him / that she liked.

연구

전치사 about의 용법

(1) There is something strange about him.
그에게는 어떤 이상한 것이 있다.

(2) There is something mystical about her beauty.
그녀의 아름다움에는 어떤 신비스러운 것이 있다.

---

4. A child / aged six / must go to school. 〔단축 관계사절〕

= (a) A child / who is aged six / must go to school.
= (b) A child, when he is aged six, must go to school.
= (c) A child must go to school when he is aged six.
= (d) When he is aged six, a child must go to school.
= (e) When a child is aged six, he must go to school.

note aged six = six years of age = six years old

---

5. Three men / pulling on the rope / couldn't lift the safe.
〔단축 관계사절〕

= (a) Three men **who** pulled on the rope couldn't lift the safe.
= (b) Three men pulled on the rope **but** couldn't lift the safe.

note lift 들어올리다 | safe 금고

---

6. Anyone / following this advice could find himself in trouble. 〔단축 관계사절〕

= (a) Anyone **who** should follow this advice **could find himself in trouble.**

= (b) Anyone **could find himself in trouble if** he should follow this advice.

note find himself in trouble = to get into trouble 곤경에 빠지다

7. An idea / that is not dangerous / is unworthy of being called an idea at all.

= (a) An idea, **if** it is not dangerous, is unworthy of being called an idea at all.

= (b) An idea is unworthy of being called an idea at all **if** it is not dangerous.

 표현

unworthy of being called an idea

= not worthy of being called an idea

= not worthy to be called an idea

= not worth the name

7.1 An education that does not meet the demands of society is not worth the name.

교육은 사회의 요구를 만족시켜주지 않는다면 교육이라고 부를 가치가 없다.

8. Milk cows / that are properly fed / can deliver up to eighty pounds of milk per day.

= (a) Milk cows, **if** they are properly fed, can deliver up to eighty pounds of milk per day.

= (b) Milk cows properly fed can deliver up to eighty pounds of milk per day.

note **properly: adequately** 제대로; 충분히 | **feed** 먹이다 | **deliver = to produce** 생산하다 | **up to** (위로 →) ~에 이르기까지; 최고 (= a maximum of ≠ at least = a minimum of 적어도; 최저) | **per day: a day** 하루에

9. A bad burn / improperly treated / may leave a scar on the skin. (단축 관계사절)

= (a) A bad burn that is improperly treated may leave a scar on the skin.
= (b) A bad burn that is not properly treated may leave a scar on the skin.
= (c) A bad burn, if it is not properly treated, may leave a scar on the skin.

note burn 화상 | treat 치료하다 | scar 흉터

10. Sometimes people / who are unable to express anger directly / do so passively by holding grudges.

= (a) Sometimes people, when they are unable to express anger directly, do so passively by holding grudges.
= (b) Sometimes when they are unable to express anger directly, people do so passively by holding grudges.
= (c) Sometimes people express anger passively by holding grudges when they are unable to do so directly.

note grudge 악의; 적대감; 원한 → hold grudges 악의를 품다

 문맥
"do so" = "express anger"
"passively" 수동적으로 = "indirectly" 간접적으로 ≠ "directly" 직접적으로

11. A self-image / long held / becomes a reality ultimately.
                                                        (단축 관계사절)

= (a) A self-image / that is long held / becomes a reality ultimately.
= (b) A self-image, if it is long held, becomes a reality ultimately.
= (c) A self-image becomes a reality ultimately if it is long held.

note self-image 자아상 | become a reality: to come true 현실이 되다 | ultimately: in the end 결국

12. A goal / worked toward half-heartedly / is seldom achieved. 〔단축 관계사절〕

🔊 순해

다음 두 번역 중 어느 것이 옳은지 생각해 보라.

(A) 마지못해 세워진 / 목적은 / 거의 성취되지 못한다.

(B) 목표는 / 그것을 이루기 위해 열심히 노력하지 않으면 / 좀처럼 성취되지 않는다.

= (a) A goal / that is worked toward half-heartedly / is seldom achieved.

= (b) A goal, if it is worked toward half-heartedly, is seldom achieved. 〔수동 구조〕

= (c) If you work toward your goal half-heartedly, you seldom achieve it. 〔능동 구조〕

note work toward = to work for ~을 위해 일하다, 노력하다 ex. The United Nations works toward world peace. | half-heartedly: without enthusiasm 열성 없이 | achieve: to accomplish 성취하다

13. A piece of iron / dipped into liquid air / becomes so brittle that it will shatter if dropped. 〔단축 관계사절〕

= (a) A piece of iron / that is dipped into liquid air / becomes so brittle that it will shatter if (it is) dropped.

= (b) A piece of iron, when it is dipped into liquid air, becomes so brittle that it will shatter if dropped.

= (c) When it is dipped into liquid air, a piece of iron becomes so brittle that it will shatter if dropped.

note dip: to immerse 담그다 | liquid air 액체 공기 | brittle: easily shattered (쉽게 부서지는 →) 부서지기 쉬운 | shatter: to break to pieces (부서져 조각이 되다 →) 산산 조각이 나다 | drop 떨어뜨리다

14. A solid / that is denser than the liquid in which it is placed / will sink, and if it is less dense than the liquid, it will float.

= (a) A solid will sink if it is denser than the liquid in which it is placed, and if it is less dense than the liquid, it will float.
= (b) When a solid is placed in a liquid, it will sink if it is denser than the liquid, and if it is less dense than the liquid, it will float.

note solid (n.) 고체 | denser 밀도가 더 큰 | place (v.): to put 넣다 | sink 가라앉다 | float 뜨다

15. Infants / who are neglected, ignored, or for any reason do not experience enough touch, / suffer mental and physical deterioration, even to the point of death.

note infant: a very young child, usually from birth to ten months 유아 | neglect: to give too little care or attention to 소홀히하다 | ignore: to pay no attention to; disregard 무시하다 | deteriorate 퇴화하다

 표현

do not experience enough touch 충분한 손댐을 경험하지 아니하다
= are not touched enough 누가 충분히 손대주지 아니하다

suffer mental and physical deterioration
= deteriorate mentally and physically 정신적으로 그리고 신체적으로 퇴화하다

to the point of death
= so far as to die 죽을 정도로 많이

Her manner of speaking is direct to the point of rudeness.
= Her manner of speaking is so direct as to be rude.
그녀의 말하는 방식은 너무도 솔직해서 무례할 정도이다.

16. Individuals / exposed to loud noise for long intervals / may suffer temporary or permanent loss of hearing. (단축 관계사절)

다음 두 번역 중 어느 것이 옳은지 생각해 보라.

(A) 개개인들은 오랫동안 커다란 소음에 노출되어 있어 일시적 혹은 영구히 청력을 잃는 시련을 겪을지도 모른다.

(B) 사람들은 / 소음에 장기간 노출되면 / 일시적으로나 영구적으로 청각을 상실할 수 있다.

= (a) Individuals who are exposed to loud noise for long intervals may ...

= (b) Individuals, when they are exposed to loud noise for long intervals, may ...

= (c) When they are exposed to loud noise for long intervals, individuals may ...

= (d) Exposed to loud noise for long intervals, individuals may ...

= (e) Exposure to loud noise for long intervals may cause temporary or permanent loss of hearing.

note individual: a person 사람 │ be exposed to ~에 노출되어 있다 │ interval = a period of time 기간 │ temporary: lasting for a short time; not permanent 일시적인

표현

suffer temporary or permanent loss of hearing 〔명사 중심의 표현〕

= lose hearing temporarily or permanently 〔동사 중심의 표현〕

---

17. Ordinary table sugar / combined with iodine / works best / to speed the healing of wounds and burns. 〔단축 관계사절〕

= (a) Ordinary table sugar that is combined with iodine works ...

= (b) Ordinary table sugar, when it is combined with iodine, works ...

= (c) When it is combined with iodine, ordinary table sugar works ...

= (d) Combined with iodine, ordinary table sugar works ...

note combine 결합하다 │ iodine 요드 │ speed (v.): to promote 촉진하다 │ heal 낫다

표현

(1) The Bible did much to mold his character.

= The Bible contributed greatly to the molding of his character.

= The Bible played a great part in the molding of his character.

성경이 그의 인격 형성에 큰 역할을 했다.

(2) His morning walks did much for his health.

= His morning walks contributed greatly to his health.

그의 아침 산책이 그의 건강에 크게 이바지했다.

(3) The decision did little to improve the situation.

그 결정은 그 사태를 개선하는 데 거의 도움이 되지 않았다.

---

18. She is given to making nasty, cruel remarks / followed by: "What's the matter; can't you take a joke?" (단축 관계사절)

= ... remarks that are followed by ...

note be given to ~하는 경향 또는 버릇이 있다 │ nasty: very unpleasant; ill-natured 매우 불쾌한; 고약한 │ cruel 잔인한 │ remark: a comment 말 │ take 받아들이다

표현

She is given to eating too much.

= She is in the habit of eating too much.

= She tends to eat too much.

18.1 Take two tablets with water, followed by one tablet every eight hours.

   = Take two tablets with water, which is to / should be followed by ...

   = Take two tablets with water, and after that, (take) one tablet every eight hours.

18.2 In these experiments, some salt-fed animals never developed hypertension / whereas a few rapidly developed very severe hypertension / followed by early death.

   = ... very severe hypertension that was followed by early death.

   = ... very severe hypertension and (subsequently) died early.

note develop 일으키다; 발생시키다 │ hypertension: high blood pressure 고혈압증 │ whereas: but; while 그러나; 반면에 │ severe: grave 심한; 중한

19. One of the most common precursors of cancer is a traumatic loss or a feeling of emptiness in one's life. When a salamander loses a limb, it grows a new one. In an analogous way, when a human being suffers an emotional loss that is not properly dealt with, the body often responds by developing a new growth. It appears that if we can react to loss with personal growth, we can prevent growth gone wrong within us.

note precursor: a harbinger 전조 | traumatic: painful 고통스러운 〈 A trauma is an experience that produces psychological injury or pain. trauma는 마음의 상처나 고통을 가져오는 경험이다. | salamander 도롱뇽 | limb: a leg 다리 | analogous: similar 유사한 → in an analogous way = similarly | emotional: psychological 심리적인 | properly: adequately 적절히 | deal with: to handle 처리하다

 문맥

"react" = "respond"

"growth gone wrong within us" = "cancer"

*The art of living lies not in eliminating
but in growing with troubles.*

- Bernard M. Baruch

5. 전치사구 ①

_ to 전치사구

❶ He escaped the danger / **to** my great relief.

= (a) He escaped the danger, **and** I was greatly relieved.
= (b) He escaped the danger, **so** (that) I was greatly relieved.
그가 그 위험을 모면해서 / 나는 크게 안심이 되었다.

❷ The film was released in America / **to** much critical acclaim.

다음 두 번역 중 어느 것이 옳은지 생각해 보라.
(A) 그 영화는 미국에서 개봉되어 많은 비판적인 칭찬을 받았다.
(B) 그 영화는 미국에서 개봉되어 평론가들로부터 많은 칭찬을 받았다.

= (a) The film was released in America. It received much acclaim from the critics.
= (b) The film was released in America **and** received much acclaim from the critics.

note release 개봉하다 | critical: of critics 평론가들의 | acclaim: praise 칭찬

❸ A nurse tended his wound, / **to** no avail; he bled **to** death.

한 간호사가 그의 상처를 돌보았으나, 아무 소용이 없었다. 그는 출혈로 사망했다.

note tend: to look after; care for 돌보다 | to no avail: to no effect; in vain 아무 소용 없는; 헛된 | **bleed to death** (피를 흘려서 / 죽다 →) 출혈로 사망하다 〈 to bleed too much and die

33

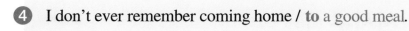

4 I don't ever remember coming home / **to** a good meal.

= (a) I don't ever remember coming home **and** having a good meal.
= (b) I don't ever remember (that) I came home **and** had a good meal.

나는 한 번도 집에 와서 좋은 식사를 해본 기억이 나지 않는다.

EXERCISE
순해순역 연습

---

1. (a) After church / we sat down / to dinner.

   (b) After years of wandering / he settled down / to a peaceful life.

(a) sat down to dinner = sat down and had dinner
(b) settled down to a peaceful life = settled down and lived peacefully

---

2. (a) The wind died away / to a dead calm.

   (b) Then, as Rosa started to sing, the noise died away / to pin-drop silence.

   (c) Bill has wasted away / to a shadow of his former self.

(a) to a dead calm = and it became dead calm

(b) to pin-drop silence
   = and came silence in which a pin might have been heard to drop 〔수동 구조〕
   = and came silence in which you might have heard a pin drop 〔능동 구조〕

(c) waste away = to become extremely thin 몹시 야위어지다
   to a shadow of his former self = and (has) become a shadow of his former self

---

3. I woke out of my deep sleep to a gradual recognition that I was at home and not in the dormitory.

to a gradual recognition = and gradually recognized

gradually: little by little; slowly 차츰: 서서히 | recognize: to realize 깨닫다 | dormitory 기숙사(격식을 차리지 않는 영어 에서는 흔히 줄여 dorm이라 한다.)

---

4. On Wednesday morning, October 10, we awoke to the ominous news that some 20 Soviet transport aircraft were on the way to Syria.

---

to the ominous news = and heard the ominous news

ominous 불길한 〈 omen 불길한 징조 | some: about; approximately 대략 | transport aircraft 수송 비행기: 수송기 | be on the way to ~로 가고 있는 중이다

---

5. Work and play are both necessary for our happiness. We should not stress the one to the exclusion of the other.

---

to the exclusion of the other = and exclude the other

stress: to emphasize 강조하다 | exclude 제외하다

---

6. (a) He smoked a lot, to the detriment of his health.

   (b) To his detriment, it must be said that he allowed the prisoners to be tortured.

(a) He smoked a lot, and caused detriment to his health.
  = He smoked a lot, which was a detriment to his health.

(b) Although it will be to his detriment, it must be said that ...
  = Although it will do him harm, it must be said that ...

note detriment: harm; damage 손해; 손상 | torture 고문하다 → torture ~ to death 고문해서 죽이다

7. (a) Knowledge and the search for knowledge have persisted through the centuries / to the enormous benefit of human beings.

   (b) We in the Western world have encouraged scientific discovery and its application intensively for 200 years / to our vast material benefits.

(a) to the enormous benefit of human beings

= and (, as a result,) have brought enormous benefits to human beings

(b) to our vast material benefits

= and (, as a result,) have brought us vast material benefits

note persist: to continue 계속되다 | through the centuries (여러 세기를 통해서 →) 인류의 역사를 통해서 | enormous: huge; vast 막대한 | application: use 이용 | intensively 집중적으로 | vast: huge; immense 막대한

8. Many people, especially men, tend to think only in terms of work-related goals, while many women tend to set goals having to do with others — such as getting a child through college or finishing a charity drive — to the exclusion of their own needs.

to the exclusion of their own needs

= and (they tend to) exclude their own needs

 표현

"think only in terms of work-related goals"

= set goals having to do only with their work

note tend to (do) (~하는) 경향이 있다 | in terms of: in relation to ~와 관련해서 | having to do with: related to ~와 관련된 | put / get ~ through college (~로 하여금 대학을 거쳐 나오게 하다 →) ~에게 대학 교육을 받게 하다 | charity drive 자선 운동

6. 전치사구 ②

_ with, without 전치사구

① Twice he followed his own advice, / **with** disastrous results.

= (a) Twice he followed his own advice, **which** brought about disastrous results.

= (b) Twice he followed his own advice, **and** the results were disastrous.

두 번 그는 자기 자신의 충고를 따랐는데, 그것은 지극히 나쁜 결과를 가져왔다.

② The manufacturer has done everything possible to upgrade his product, / **with** the result that it is now of excellent quality.

= (a) The manufacturer has done everything possible to upgrade his product. The result is that it is now of excellent quality.

= (b) The manufacturer has done everything possible to upgrade his product. As a result, it is now of excellent quality.

그 제조업자는 모든 가능한 일을 해서 자기 제품의 질을 향상시켜와서, 그 결과 지금 그것은 품질이 우수하다.

note manufacture 제조하다 | product 제품 | upgrade: to improve the quality of ~의 질을 향상시키다 | excellent: outstandingly good 뛰어나게 훌륭한: 우수한

③ If you think you can commit a crime / **without** getting caught, you are a fool.

다음 두 번역 중 어느 것이 합리적인지 생각해 보라.

(A) 만일 발각되지 않고 죄를 지을 수 있다고 네가 생각한다면, 너는 바보다.

(B) 만일 네가 죄를 짓고도 / 발각되지 않을 수 있으리라 생각한다면, 너는 바보다.

죄를 짓는 행위가 발각되는 것에 선행하므로 필자는 (B)가 합리적이라 생각한다.

= If you think you can commit a crime **and** will not get caught, you are a fool.

---

4 Facts may be known in prodigious numbers / **without** the knowers of them loving wisdom.

= (a) Facts may be known in prodigious numbers **but** the knowers of them may not love wisdom. 〔수동 구조+능동 구조〕

= (b) One may know facts in prodigious numbers **but** one may not love wisdom. 〔능동 구조+능동 구조〕

〔직역〕 사람은 아는 것은 많으나 지혜는 사랑하지 않을 수 있다.

〔취지〕 사람은 아는 것이 많다고 해서 반드시 지혜로운 것은 아니다.

= The person who has a lot of knowledge is not necessarily wise.

[note] prodigious: very great; huge; vast 매우 많은: 거대한: 방대한

The applause of a single human being
is of great consequence.

EXERCISE
순해순역 연습

1. I've tried to interest him in any number of activities, **with** little success.

= I've tried to interest him in any number of activities, **but** I've had little success.

note any number of: numerous; many 수많은: 많은

2. I had been puzzling over the problem for over an hour / without any result, / when all at once the solution flashed across my mind.

= I had been puzzling over the problem for over an hour **but** I had not had any result, and then all at once the solution flashed across my mind.

note puzzle over: to think hard about ~에 대해서 열심히 생각하다 | all at once: all of a sudden; suddenly 갑자기

표현
An idea flashed across my mind.
= An idea occurred to me like a flash.
= I lit upon an idea.
어떤 생각이 섬광처럼 내 머릿속에 떠올랐다.

3. The most beautiful discovery / true friends make / is / that they can grow separately / **without** growing apart.

grow separately 따로-각자-성장하다 | grow apart 갈라지다; 사이가 멀어지다

 관찰

separately와 apart는 비슷한 뜻을 갖고 있으나 grow와 결합해 각기 다른 뜻을 갖게 됨으로써 주어진 문장에 시적인 아름다움을 부여해 준다. (오, 여러분이 이런 언어의 아름다움을 느낄 수 있다면!)

4. When Buddhism first reached China from India, **with** revolutionary results, it underwent a slow but far-reaching transformation through Taoism.

Buddhism 불교 | revolutionary: completely new and different 혁명적인 | undergo: to go through; experience 겪다; 경험하다 | far-reaching: extensive 광범위한 | transformation: a change 변화 | Taoism 도교

표현

underwent a slow but far-reaching transformation (명사 중심의 표현)
= was transformed slowly but far-reachingly (동사 중심의 표현)

5. I was just sitting down to dinner / when Tom phoned / **with** the sad news.

= I was just sitting down to dinner when Tom phoned **and** told me the sad news.

6. Our dog was something of a slow learner. The whole family had to pitch in / with expressions of approval and commendation / before he got the idea.

note something of a slow learner: rather a slow learner; quite a slow learner │ pitch in: to join in 끼여 들다; 가담하다 │ approval 인정 │ commendation: praise 칭찬

순해

pitch in **with** expressions of approval and commendation

(A) 인정하고 칭찬하는 표정으로 / 끼여들다 [재래식]

(B) 끼여들어서 / 인정하고 칭찬하는 표정을 짓다 [김영로식]

= pitch in **and** make expressions of approval and commendation

7. Although adult children sometimes come home to Mom and Dad, middle-aged and elderly people seldom move in with their grown children. Older people take pride in their independence, enjoy their freedom, and do not want to be a burden to their children.

note move in with 옮겨 들어가서 ~와 살다 │ middle-aged 중년의 │ elderly: in old age; aged 노년의; 연로한 │ take pride in: to be proud of; pride oneself on ~에 대해서 자랑스럽게 생각하다 │ burden 짐; 부담

문맥

"grown children" = "adult children" 성장한 자식들

"Older people" = "middle-aged and elderly people"

"come home to" = "move in with"

8. It has been noticed in school / that if children / who are lacking in confidence / are given an opportunity / to excel in one area / then the confidence / that is built up / extends to other areas / with a marked improvement in performance.

note notice: to observe 관찰하다 | be lacking in: to be wanting in; be deficient in; be short of ~가 부족하거나 없다 | build up: to increase or strengthen 증가시키거나 강화시키다

If you treat an individual as he is, he will stay that way.
But if you treat him as if he were what he could be,
he will become what he could be.

- Goethe

7. 전치사구 ③

_ for, at, in 전치사구

① Take the dog / **for** a run.

순해

다음 두 번역을 비교해 보라.

(A) 달리게 하기 위해 / 개를 데리고 가거라. 〔재래식〕

(B) 개를 데리고 가서 / 달리게 해라. 〔김영로식〕

필자는 주어진 문장은 다음이 발전해서 이루어진 형태라 보기 때문에 (B)가 합리적이라고 생각한다.

= Take the dog **and** run him / her.

② The self-made millionaire avoids limousines / **for** buses.

= The self-made millionaire avoids limousines **and** takes buses.

그 자수성가한 백만장자는 리무진을 피하고 / 버스를 탄다.

note self-made 자수성가한 | millionaire 백만장자 → billionaire 억만장자

③ The poor fox escaped from the trap **at** the cost of a leg.

= The poor fox escaped from the trap **but** lost a leg.

그 가엾은 여우는 덫에서 빠져 나왔으나 / 다리 하나를 잃었다.

cf To enlarge the automobile plant, they had to divert a nearby river — at a cost of $1.7 billion.

그 자동차 공장을 확장하기 위해, 근처에 있는 강줄기를 다른 곳으로 돌려야 했는데 — 비용은 17억 달러가 들었다.

4 Calcium, the most abundant mineral in the body, works with phosphorus / **in** maintaining bones and teeth.

= Calcium, the most abundant mineral in the body, works with phosphorus / to maintain bones and teeth.

칼슘은 신체 안에 있는 가장 풍부한 광물질인데, 인과 협동하여 / 뼈와 치아를 유지한다.

note abundant: very plentiful 풍부한 | phosphorus 인 | maintain 유지하다

I learned it is through giving
that we receive the worthwhile things of life.

- Peace Pilgrim

EXERCISE
순해순역 연습

※ 다음 밑줄 친 부분들을 접속사를 이용해서 바꾸어 써보라.
(2, 7, 8번은 번역만 하시오.)

1. A: I've been thinking about my mother a lot today.
    B: Why not go over / for a visit?

note Why not ~? = Why don't you ~? (상대방에게 '제의' 하는 표현)

2. After a short pause / for a sip of water, the speaker went on / to discuss the habits of lions in the wild.

note take a sip of ~을 한 모금 마시다 | go on to (do) 계속해서 (하다) | the wild: natural habitat 자연 서식지

3. Consequently, after World War I increasing numbers of spectators deserted the theater / for the movies.

note consequently: as a result 그 결과로 | spectator 관객 | desert: to leave; abandon 떠나다: 버리다

 순해

desert A / for B

46

(A) B를 위해 / A를 버리다 [재래식]

(B) A를 버리고 / B로 가다 (또는 B를 택하다) [김영로식]

4. At an alarming rate, West European high school students have been dropping German / in favor of English, mainly because they believe English is easier to learn.

`note` at an alarming rate = alarmingly 놀라울 정도로

5. When a question is complicated, don't give the first answer / that comes to mind. Take time / for reflection.

`note` complicated: complex 복잡한 ｜ reflection: careful thinking 숙고

 표현

자동 표현과 타동 표현

1. (a) come to mind 머릿속에 떠오르다 [자동 표현]
   (b) bring to mind 머릿속에 떠오르게 하다 [타동 표현]
2. (a) come about 발생하다
   (b) bring about 발생하게 하다

6. A female toad / listening to male love calls / scorns the tenors / in favor of the basses.

= (a) A female toad / that listens to male love calls / scorns the tenors / in favor of the basses.

= (b) A female toad, / when she listens to male love calls, / scorns the tenors / in favor of the basses.

순해

scorn A / in favor of B

(A) B를 위해 / A를 배척하다 (재래식)

(B) A를 배척하고 / B를 좋아하다 (김영로식)

---

7. (a) People usually become famous / at the cost of their privacy.

   (b) Knowledge is gained / at the cost of innocence.

(a) = When people become famous, they usually lose their privacy.

(b) = One gains knowledge at the cost of one's innocence. (능동 구조)
   = When one gains knowledge, one loses one's innocence.

---

8 (a) Civilization today depends on wood, at great cost to the world's natural resources.

   (b) Protectionism may provide short-term benefits to special interests but at much greater costs to the rest of society.

(a) = Civilization today depends on wood, and causes great loss to the world's natural resources.
   = Civilization today depends on wood, causing great loss to the world's natural resources.

(b) = Protectionism may provide short-term benefits to special interests but causes much greater loss to the rest of society.

EXERCISE
종합 연습문제

1. (a) Words / once spoken / can never be recalled.

   (b) As a rule, language / once within our control / can be employed for oral or written purposes.

2. A man travels the world over / in search of what he needs / and returns home / to find it.

이 문장에는 다음 네 가지 동작이 들어 있다.

1) A man travels the world over (= A man travels over the world).
2) He searches for what he needs.
3) He returns home.
4) He finds it.

3. Machine after machine appears in a rapid succession, each replacing its predecessor, working for a time and giving way to still better devices.

"predecessor" = 'preceding machine' 그 이전의 기계
"give way to" = 'be replaced by' ~로 대치되다
"devices" = 'machines'

---

4. Most of us spend fifty-nine minutes an hour / living in the past / with regret for lost joys / or shame for things badly done, / or in a future / which we either long for / or dread.

이 문장에는 다음 주요 동작들이 들어 있다.

1) Most of us spend fifty-nine minutes an hour.
2) live in the past and
3) feel regret for lost joys
4) or (feel) shame for things badly done
5) or (live) in a future / which we either long for
6) or dread

note long for: to want very much; yearn for 갈망하다 | dread: to fear greatly 무척 두려워하다

---

5. No matter how well a student may know a language, he cannot read in that language / with good comprehension / if the subject of the text is one / he knows absolutely nothing about / and therefore can have no real interest in.

read ... with good comprehension
= read ... and comprehend well

 구문

기본 구조와 파생 구조

(a) I know nothing about the subject. (기본)

나는 그 문제에 대해서 아무 것도 아는 것이 없다.

(b) The subject is one (that) I know nothing about. 〔파생〕

그 문제는 내가 아는 것이 아무 것도 없는 문제이다.

---

6. The greenback's value plunged near last August's record
   low of 152.55 yen to the dollar / before recovering slightly
   / to close in Tokyo at 153.1.

🎧 순해

다음 두 번역 중 어느 것이 합리적인지 생각해 보라.

(A) 미국 달러의 시세는 지난 8월의 기록적인 최저였던 1달러에 152.55엔 가까이 갑
자기 떨어졌다가 / 약간 회복해서 / 도쿄에서 마감했을 때에는 153.1엔이었다.

(B) 미국 달러의 시세는 / 1달러에 153.1엔으로 도쿄에서 마감하기 위해 / 약간 회복
하기 전에 / 지난 8월의 기록적인 최저였던 152.55엔 가까이로 갑자기 떨어졌다.

주어진 문장은 다음 세 문장을 결합한 것이라 볼 수 있다.

1) The greenback's value plunged near last August's record low of 152.55 yen
   to the dollar.
2) It recovered slightly.
3) It closed in Tokyo at 153.1.

note   greenback: U.S. dollar ｜ plunge: to decline quickly and suddenly 빠르게 그리고 갑자기 떨어지다 ｜
record low 기록적인 최저치 ≠ record high

---

7. To earn a bit more money / he decided to try his hand at
   novel writing. Two stories of Irish life appeared / without
   much success or acclaim, / to be followed by a historical
   novel / that sank / without trace.

---

note   earn money: to make money 돈을 벌다 ｜ a bit: a little 조금 ｜ try one's hand at ~에 손을 대보다 → try
one's luck at ~에 자신의 운을 시험해 보다 ｜ novel 소설 → historical novel 역사 소설 ｜ acclaim: praise;
applause 칭찬; 갈채 ｜ sink 가라앉다 ｜ trace 자취; 흔적

8. Of the many wonders of nature, so familiar that they pass almost unnoticed, water is one. In all its changes, it is never lost, / disappearing / only to appear again in another form / in the constant service of nature and civilization.

두 번째 문장에는 다음 다섯 가지 동작이 들어 있다.

1) it changes
2) it is never lost
3) it disappears
4) it only appears again in another form
5) it constantly serves nature and civilization

그리고 in the constant service of nature and civilization은 다음 두 가지 방법으로 바꾸어 쓸 수 있다.

(a) (in order) to constantly serve nature and civilization
(b) and constantly serves nature and civilization

🗺 어순

(a) Water is one / of the many wonders of nature, (which are) so familiar that they pass almost unnoticed. 〔기본〕

(b) Of the many wonders of nature, so familiar that they pass almost unnoticed, water is one. 〔변형〕

👆 표현

1. pass unnoticed
= go unnoticed
= are not noticed 〔수동 구조〕
= we do not notice 〔능동 구조〕

2. He passed unrecognized because of his disguise.
= He was not recognized because of his disguise.
= They did not recognize him because he was in disguise.
사람들은 그를 알아보지 못했는데, 그것은 그가 변장했기 때문이었다.

8. 올려번역이 가져오는 몇 가지 문제점

우리나라 사람들이 영어를 대할 때에 저지르는 중요한 잘못이나 어색함은 많은 경우에 영어를 거꾸로 따져 올라오는 데서 나온다고 필자는 생각한다. 여기서 몇 가지 예를 살펴보기로 하자.

다음 각 예문 밑에 있는 두 번역 중 어느 것이 옳거나 합리적인지 생각해 보라.

① **Journalism has been a continuing schooling** / that I got paid for.

(A) 언론업은 / 내가 그 대가로 봉급을 받은 / 계속적인 학교 교육이었다.
(B) 언론업이 내게는 계속해서 학교 교육 같은 역할을 해왔는데, / 그런데도 나는 (수업료를 내기는커녕 도리어) 거기에 종사하는 대가로 봉급을 받았다.

(A)에서는 '그 대가'가 무엇에 대한 대가인지 분명하지 않을 뿐만 아니라, 이 문장 전체의 의미가 분명하지 않다(안타깝게도, 우리는 영어를 한국어로 옮겨놓은 책에서 이런 말이 아닌 말을 흔히 볼 수 있다). (B)는 새로운 방식의 필자의 번역이다.

주어진 문장은 다음과 같이 바꾸어 쓸 수 있다.

Journalism has been a continuing schooling for me; nevertheless I got paid for engaging in it.

note schooling: education received at school 학교에서 받는 교육 | pay for ~에 대해 (봉급·가격·대가 따위를) 지불하다

② **Questions of educations are frequently discussed** / as if they bore no relation to the social system / in which and for which the education is carried on.

(A) 교육 문제들이, / 그 안에서 또 그것을 위해 행해지는 / 사회 조직과는 관계가 없는 것처럼 / 논의되는 적이 많다. 〔어느 책의 번역〕

(B) 교육 문제들이 / 자주 논의되고 있으나, / 마치 그것들이 사회 체제와 아무 관계가 없는 것처럼, / 일정한 사회 체제 안에서 그리고 그 사회 체제를 위해서 교육은 실시된다. 〔김영로식〕

(A)에서는 '그'와 '그것'이 무엇을 가리키는지 알 수 없다. 이들이 뒤에 나오는 '사회 조직'을 가리킨다는 주장은 억지이다. 왜냐하면 한국어에는 이런 대명사 용법이 없기 때문이다.

🖐 표현

명사 중심의 표현과 동사(또는 형용사) 중심의 표현

1. bear no relation to (=have no relation to)
= be not related to ~와 관계가 없다
2. bear some similarity to (=have some similarity to)
= be somewhat similar to ~와 다소 비슷하다
3. He bears a close resemblance to his father.
= He resembles his father closely. 그는 자기 아버지를 많이 닮았다.

③ Acids are chemical compounds / that, in water solution, have a sharp taste, a corrosive action on metals, and the ability to turn certain blue vegetable dyes red.

(A) 산이란 / 신랄한 맛과 금속을 부식시키는 작용을 가지며, 어떤 잎 푸른 채소를 붉은 색으로 물들이는 능력을 가진 용액 상태의 / 화학적 혼합물이다. 〔어느 책의 번역〕

(B) 산은 화학적 혼합물인데, / **수용액 상태일 때는**(=물에 용해되어 있을 때는), 신맛이 나고, 금속을 부식시키는 작용을 하며, 그리고 어떤 청색 식물 염료를 붉게 변화시킬 수 있다. 〔필자의 번역〕

산은 '용액 상태의' 화학적 혼합물이 아니므로 (A)는 오역이다. 이것은 '올려번역'이 가져오는 중대한 잘못이다.

in water solution (부사구)

= when they are dissolved in water (부사절)

note acid 산 | chémical 화학적 〈 chemistry | compound 혼합물 | solution 용액 〈 dissolve 용해시키다: 용해되다 | sharp: sour 신 | corrosive 부식시키는 〈 corrode 부식시키다 | action 작용 | dye 염료 | turn: to change

④ About three thousand years ago, North Americans began to craft clay pots, / an innovation that accompanied the appearance of agriculture in the eastern area of the continent.

(A) 북아메리카 사람들은 / 대륙의 동부 지역에 출현한 농경과 함께 새로운 기술 혁신인 / 점토 항아리를 약 3,000년 전에 정교하게 만들기 시작했다. (어느 책의 번역)

(B) 약 3,000년 전에, 북아메리카 사람들은 점토 항아리를 만들기 시작했는데, / 이것은 북미대륙의 동부 지역에서 출현한 농경에 수반한 새로운 발명품이었다. (필자의 번역)

note craft (v.): to make 만들다 | clay 점토: 흙 | pot 항아리 | innovation: a new invention 새로운 발명품 | accompany: to happen along with ~와 함께 발생하다: 수반하다

이 문장의 마지막 부분(an innovation ... continent)은 바로 앞에 있는 clay pots를 설명해 주는 동격구이다. 다음 예를 보라.

4.1 Last year 97 students died of measles, an illness that could have been prevented with a single shot.

작년에 97명의 학생들이 홍역으로 죽었는데, 이 병은 단 한 번의 주사로 막을 수 있었을 것이다.

Nothing in the world can take the place of persistence.
Talent will not; nothing is more common than
unsuccessful men of talent.
Genius will not...
The world is full of educated derelicts.
Persistence and determination alone are omnipotent.
The slogan "PRESS ON" has solved and always will
solve the problems of the human race.

- Calvin Coolidge
(30th president of the United States of America)

part 2

영어의 서술 방식

그런식으로
전개 하면
배가 산으로
간다구~!

영차!
영차!

1. 서론

영어에서 어떤 정보(information)를 문장의 형태로 전달하는 방법에는 다음 네 가지 특징들이 있는 것 같다.

첫째, 영어의 서술 방식은 마치 차례차례 따져나가는 수사관의 심문에 대한 답을 엮어 놓은 것과 비슷하다. 다음 예문을 보라.

① He / hit / her / on the head.

1) 누가? ······················· He (그가)
2) 무엇을 했나? ··············· hit (때렸다)
3) 누구를? ····················· her (그녀를)
4) 어디에 (말이냐)? ··········· on the head (머리 위에)

1.1 He is blind in one eye. 그는 한쪽 눈이 보이지 않는다.
1.2 He kissed her on the lips. 그는 그녀의 입술에 키스했다.
1.3 He patted me on the back. 그는 내 등을 두드려주었다.
1.4 He kicked me in the leg. 그는 내 다리를 찼다.

둘째, 영어에서는 문장의 뼈대 구조를 문장의 앞부분에 제시하는 경향이 있다. 이것은 정보를 받는 사람의 이해를 돕기 위해 만들어진 장치인 것 같다.

② It is not easy / to get a taxi in Seoul at rush hours.

그것은 쉽지 않다 / 서울에서 러시 아워에 택시를 잡는 것 말이다.

이것을 다음과 비교해 보라.

(a) To get a taxi in Seoul at rush hours / is not easy.

일반적으로, 영어는 앞의 예문 2와 같은 문장을 좋아하고, (2a)와 같은 문장은 싫어한다. 전자(the former)에서는 문장의 뼈대 구조가 빨리 파악되고, 따라서, 그 의미도 빨리 파악되기 때문이리라 필자는 생각한다.

셋째, 영어에서는 뼈대를 이루는 정보는 문장의 앞부분에 내세우고, 그것을 설명하거나 수식하는 말은 뒤로 돌린다.

❸ This is the **book** / he talked about yesterday.

이것이 그 책이다 / 그가 어제 얘기하던 것 말이다.

= (a) This is the book / about which he talked yesterday. (formal)
= (b) This is the book / (which) he talked about yesterday. (informal)
= (c) This is the book / (that) he talked about yesterday. (informal)

넷째, 영어에는 앞에 나온 말의 일부를 보충해 주거나, 일부 또는 전부를 달리 설명해 주는 말들이 매우 발달해 있다.

❹
(a) He seldom, if ever, goes to church.
(b) You must help them, and that at once.
(c) Taking notes, even incomplete ones, is usually more efficient than relying on one's memory.
(d) She wore a strange smile on her face, a smile that said many things.
(e) During the 1980's, the cost of a college education rose almost 8% to 10% a year, about twice the rate of inflation.

(a) = He seldom goes to church if he ever does.

그는 교회에 가는 일이 드물다, 설사 가는 일이 있다고 하더라도.

(b) = You must help them, and help them at once.

너는 그들을 도와야 한다, 그것도 당장 말이다.

(c) = Taking notes, even though they are incomplete ones, is usually more efficient than relying on one's memory.

노트를 하는 것이, 비록 그것이 불완전하더라도, 일반적으로 더 효과적이다, 자신의 기억에 의존하는 것보다 말이다.

(d) = She wore a strange smile on her face, and the smile said many things.

그녀는 이상한 미소를 얼굴에 띠고 있었는데, 그 미소는 많은 것을 얘기해 주었다.

(e) = During the 1980's, the cost of a college education rose almost 8% to 10% a year, and this rate (of increase) was about twice that of inflation.

1980년대에, 대학 교육 비용은 1년에 거의 8% 내지 10% 올랐는데, 이 인상률은 물가 상승률의 거의 두 배였다.

note   at once: immediately 당장 ∣ take notes 노트를 하다 ∣ efficient: effective 효과적인 ∣ rely on: to depend on ~에 의존하다 ∣ wear a smile 미소를 띠다

Our greatest glory is not in never failing,
but in rising every time we fail.

- Confucius

2. 따져나가는 논리

영어에서 하나의 문장이 만들어지는 과정은 차례차례 따져보면 다음과 같다.

①
There is no doubt — 의심할 여지가 없다 → (무엇에 대하여 말이냐?)
of his guilt — 그가 유죄라는 데 대하여

→ There is no doubt / of his guilt.

= There is no doubt / that he is guilty.

②
There is no evidence — 증거가 없다 → (무엇에 대하여 말이냐?)
of his having stolen the money — 그가 그 돈을 훔쳤다는 데 대하여

→ There is no evidence / of his having stolen the money.

=There is no evidence / that he stole the money.

③
There's a pile — 더미가 있다(쌓여 있다) → (무슨 더미 말이냐?)
of dirty clothes — 더러운 옷의 → (어디에 말이냐?)
in the corner of your room — 네 방 구석에 (말이다)

→ There's a pile / of dirty clothes / in the corner of your room.

It is not wise — 그것은 현명하지 않다 → (무엇이 말이냐?)
to mock that — 그런 것을 비웃는 것 (말이다) → (어떤 것 말이냐?)

4 of which you know so little — 거기에 대해 네가 알고 있는 것이 너무도 적은 것 (말이다)

→ It is not wise / to mock that / of which you know so little.

= It is not wise / to mock / what you know so little.

It is only that — 오로지 그런 것뿐이다 → (어떤 것 말이냐?)
which cannot be expressed otherwise — 다른 방법으로 표현할 수 없는 것 → (그것이 어떻다는 말이냐?)

5 that is worth expressing in music — 음악으로 표현할 가치가 있는 것은

→ It is only that / which cannot be expressed otherwise / that is worth expressing in music.

= It is only / what cannot be expressed in other ways / that is worth expressing in music.

이 문장의 기본형은 다음과 같다.

(5a) Only that / which cannot be expressed otherwise / is worth expressing in music.

Their ideas were criticized — 그들의 사상은 비판을 받았다 → (왜?)
as being immoral and dangerous — 부도덕하고 위험하다는 이유로 (말이다)

6 → Their ideas were criticized / as being immoral and dangerous.

= Their ideas were criticized / as they were immoral and dangerous.

7

Bill was tense — 빌은 안절부절 못했다 → (왜?)

from lack of sleep — 잠이 부족했기 때문에 (말이다)

→ Bill was tense / from lack of sleep.

= Bill was tense / because he had not had enough sleep.

8

My aunt is often confused with my mother.

— 나의 이모님을 사람들은 종종 나의 어머니와 혼동한다 → (어째서?)

whom she resembles closely — 나의 어머니를 이모님이 많이 닮았기 때문이다

→ My aunt is often confused with my mother, / whom she resembles closely.

= My aunt is often confused with my mother, / for she resembles her sister closely.

🗝 **주의**

여기서 aunt란 말을 '숙모' 라고 하지 않고 '이모' 라고 옮긴 이유는 '어머니' 를 닮을 가능성이 높은 것은 후자라고 생각되기 때문이다.

9

Today, the people once called American Indians prefer to be called Native Americans, — 오늘날, 그 사람들은 한때는 미국 인디언이라 불리었으나 미국 원주민이라 불리기를 좋아한다 → (왜?)

a name that reminds the world that they were the first people to live in the Americas — 이 이름은 세상 사람들에게 자기들이 최초로 미주에 산 사람들이라는 것을 상기시켜주기 때문이다.

→ Today, the people once called American Indians prefer to be called Native Americans, / a name that reminds the world that they were the first people to live in the Americas.

It is difficult to talk about the arts without beginning in New York or London, — 예술에 관해 얘기할 때 뉴욕이나 런던에서 시작하지 않기는 어렵다 → (왜?)

⑩ cities synonymous with the theater. — 이들 도시는 연극과 동의어이기 때문이다

→ It is difficult to talk about the arts without beginning in New York or London, / cities synonymous with the theater.

📖 **문법**

예문 9에서 a name ... Americas는 Native Americans를 설명해 주는 말이고, 예문 10에서 cities ... theater는 New York or London을 설명해 주는 말인데, 문법학자들은 이런 말들을 appositive phrases(동격구)라고 부른다.

It is a good policy to strike while the iron is hot.
It is better still to make the iron hot by striking.

- Ernest Hemingway

EXERCISE
순해순역 연습

1. There is always the danger / of the nuclear waste leaking very gradually from the containers / in which it is stored.

= There is always the danger / that the nuclear waste will leak very gradually from the containers / in which it is stored.

note nuclear waste 핵폐기물 | leak: to escape 누출되다 | gradually: little by little; slowly 조금씩: 서서히 | container 용기 | store: to keep 저장하다

2. There are many books / of which you cannot get the full value / on a single reading.

= (a) There are many books / the full value of which you cannot get / on a single reading.
= (b) There are many books / whose full value you cannot get / on a single reading.

 구문
on a single reading = by reading them only once (구)
= if you read them only once (절)

3. Education is that / which remains / when one has forgotten everything / he learned in school. –Albert Einstein

= Education is what remains when one has forgotten everything he learned in school.

---

4. It is not the man / who has too little / who is poor, but the one / who craves more.

= It is not the man / who has too little / but the one who craves more / who is poor. (기본 어순)

note crave = to want to have 갖고 싶어하다

이 문장의 기본형은 다음과 같다.

= (a) The man who has too little is not poor, but the one who craves more is.
= (b) The man who craves more is poor, but not the one who has too little.

---

5. It is not too much to say / that reading without thinking is just like eating without chewing.

표현

It is not too much to say that ~
= It is not an exaggeration to say that ~
~라고 말해도 지나치지 않다

---

6. There is no expedient / to which a man will not resort / to avoid the real labor of thinking.

= A man will resort to every expedient / to avoid the real labor of thinking.

note expedient: a means to an end 어떤 목적에 대한 수단 | resort to: to turn to ~ for help; use ~에 의존하다;
이용하다 *ex.* Never resort to violence.

 연구

There is no rule that does not have exceptions. 〔부정 중심의 표현〕

= There is no rule but has exceptions. 〔부정 중심의 표현〕

= There is no rule without exceptions. 〔부정 중심의 표현〕

= Every rule has exceptions. 〔긍정 중심의 표현〕

   (A) 예외 없는 규칙은 없다.

= (B) 모든 규칙에는 예외가 있다.

---

7. There are few things / more important for one's happiness / than to form a habit / of taking a cheerful view / of the circumstances / in which one is placed.

= There are few things / more important for one's happiness / than to form a habit / of viewing one's circumstances cheerfully.

 표현

명사 중심의 표현과 동사 중심의 표현

1. They **take** a gloomy view of the future.
   = They view the future gloomily.

   그들은 미래를 비관적으로 본다.

2. It is not always easy to **make** a clear distinction between fact and fiction.
   = It is not always easy to distinguish clearly between fact and fiction.

   사실과 허구를 명확히 구분하기는 언제나 쉽지는 않다.

3. Power **has** a tendency to corrupt.
   = Power tends to corrupt. 권력은 부패하기 쉽다.

4. He **bears** a close resemblance to his father.
   = He resembles his father closely.

이런 명사 중심의 표현에서 가장 많이 사용되는 동사는 take, make, have이다.

구문 또는 표현의 간소화

  (a) This is the circumstances / in which we are placed.

= (b) This is the circumstances / we are placed in.

= (c) This is our circumstances.

　　　이것이 우리의 사정이다.

---

8. The only thing / which makes it possible / to regard this world / we live in / without disgust / is the beauty / which now and then men create / out of the chaos.

---

note   now and then: occasionally; once in a while; at times 가끔; 때때로 | regard: to view 보다 | disgust: a strong dislike 혐오감 | create: to make 만들다; 창조하다 | chaos: confusion; disorder 혼돈; 무질서

순해

regard this world we live in / without disgust

(A) 혐오감 없이 / 우리가 사는 이 세상을 바라보다 [재래식 번역]

(B) 우리가 사는 이 세상을 바라보면서 / 혐오감을 느끼지 않다 [김영로식 번역]

= regard this world we live in / and do not feel disgust

---

9. There is a question / about the extent / to which any one of us can be free of a prejudiced view / in the area of religion.

문제

다음 두 번역 중 어느 것이 바람직한지 생각해 보라.

(A) 종교 분야에서 편견으로부터 우리들 중 누구든지 해방될 수 있는 정도에 대해서 의문이 있다.

(B) 우리가 종교 분야에서 어느 정도까지 편견으로부터 벗어날 수 있는지는 의문스럽다.

10. Although there are cultures / in which women dominate the home, America is conspicuous / for the extent / to which women have set the style of the home.

note culture: a society 사회 | dominate: to control or rule 지배하다 | conspicuous: outstanding; striking
두드러진 | set: to determine 결정하다

문제

다음 두 번역 가운데서 어느 것이 좋은지 생각해 보라.

(A) 비록 여성들이 가정을 지배하는 사회가 있지만, 미국은 여성들이 가정의 스타일을 결정해 온 정도로 두드러진다.

(B) 비록 여성들이 가정을 지배하는 사회가 있지만, 미국은 두드러지게 많이 여성들이 가정의 스타일을 결정해왔다.

참고

(1) He was conspicuous for his bravery.

= He was conspicuously brave.
그는 두드러지게 용감했다.

(2) I was surprised at the extent of his knowledge.

= I was surprised that his knowledge was very extensive.
나는 그의 지식이 광범위한 데에 놀랐다.

11. Few people will admit to being superstitious; it implies naïveté or ignorance.

= Few people will admit / that they are superstitious, for it implies / that they are naive or ignorant.

note be superstitious = to believe in superstitions 미신을 믿다 | imply: to indicate indirectly; suggest; mean 암시하다; 의미하다 | naïve: simple; childlike 단순한; 순진한 | ignorance: lack of knowledge, education, etc. 무식, 무지

12. Opera singers tone down their performances for the television cameras; effective stage acting looks exaggerated and ludicrous on the small screen.

힌트

semicolon을 중심으로 그 앞과 뒤에 주어져 있는 두 정보 사이의 논리적 관계(the logical relationship)를 생각하라.

문맥

"tone down" (본래의 뜻) 톤을 낮추다 / (문맥 속에서의 뜻) 연기의 농도를 낮추다

'performance' = "acting" 연기

"the small screen" = 'the television screen'

note exaggerated: overdone; excessive 과장된; 지나친 | ludicrous: ridiculous 우스꽝스러운

13. The best alternative to oil, coal, and nuclear reactors is solar energy, **which** is abundant, non-polluting, and potentially cheap.

note an alternative to ~을 대체(대신)할 수 있는 것 | nuclear reactor 원자로 | solar: of the sun 태양의 | abundant: plentiful 풍부한 | non-polluting: not polluting the environment 자연 환경을 오염시키지 않는 | potentially 잠재적으로

힌트

논리적 관계를 생각하라.

14. There is nothing / that helps a man in his conduct through life / more than a knowledge of his own characteristic weakness, **which**, guarded against, becomes his strength.

note in his conduct through life = in his going through life 그가 인생을 살아가는 데에 | characteristic: typical 독특한; 전형적인 | weakness 약점 | guard against ~에 대해서 경계하다

 구문

A person's weakness, guarded against, becomes his strength.
= A person's weakness, if it is guarded against, becomes his strength.
= A person's weakness becomes his strength if it is guarded against. (수동 구조)
= A person's weakness becomes his strength if he guards against it. (능동 구조)
어떤 사람의 약점은, 만일 그가 거기에 대해서 경계하면, 자신의 강점이 된다.

15. It is from the great books / that have stood the test of time / that we shall get, not only the most lasting pleasure, / but also a standard / by which to measure / our own thoughts, the thoughts of others, and the excellence of the literature of our day.

note stand the test of time 세월의 시련을 견디다: to last for a very long time 아주 오래 지속하다 | lasting: enduring 지속적인 | excellence 우수성 | literature (문맥 속에서의 뜻) = books

 구문

a standard by which to measure ...
= a standard by which we can measure ...

16. The obvious answer / to the question / how we know / about the experiences of others / is / that they are communicated to us, / either through their natural manifestations / in the form of gestures, tears, laughter, play of feature and so forth, / or by the use of language.

note obvious: clear 분명한 | communicate: to convey 전달하다 | manifestation: expression 표현 | play of feature: an expression of the face 얼굴 표정 | and so forth: etc. …등등, 따위

연구

전치사 용법의 규칙성

의미나 종류가 비슷한 말 뒤에는 같은 전치사가 온다.

(1) a road to
    a path to
    an avenue to
    a shortcut to
    an entrance to

(2) a solution to
    an answer to
    a clue to
    an approach to

(3) an obstacle to
    a barrier to
    a deterrent to
    an impediment to
    a stumbling block to

(1)의 명사들이 물리적인 의미에서의 '길'이라면, (2)의 명사들은 추상적인 의미에서의 '길'이고, (3)의 명사들은 ~로 가는 길을 막는 '장애물들'이다. 길이 목적지에 이르게 해주는 것이라면, 장애물은 목적지에 이르지 못하게 막는 것이므로 후자는 전자와 대립되는 개념이라고 볼 수 있다. 그러므로 이들 뒤에 같은 전치사가 오는 것은 당연한 것 같다.

3. 뼈대구조 먼저 제시 ①

_ 주어나 목적어에 딸린 수식 구나 절을 떼어서 문장 끝으로 이동시킨다

뼈대 구조를 문장의 앞부분에 제시하는 것은 이해를 빠르게 하기 위한 방편으로 생각되는데, 그러기 위해 다음 세 가지 방법들이 사용된다.

1. 주어나 목적어에 딸린 수식 구나 절을 떼어서 문장 끝으로 이동시킨다.
2. 짧은 요소는 앞으로, 긴 요소는 뒤로 이동시킨다.
3. 예비 주어나 예비 목적어 it을 사용한다.

❶
(a) All of us except the captain **were frightened.** [이동 전]
→ (b) All of us **were frightened** / except the captain. [이동 후]

(a) 선장을 제외한 우리들 모두는 겁이 났다.
(b) 우리들 모두는 겁이 났다, 선장은 제외하고 (말이다).

색 글자 부분은 주어 **All of us**를 수식하는 전치사구이다.

❷
(a) A rumor that he was secretly engaged to her **circulated.**
→ (b) A rumor **circulated** / that he was secretly engaged to her.

(a) 그가 남몰래 그녀와 약혼했다는 소문이 떠돌아다녔다.
(b) 소문이 떠돌아다녔다, 그가 남몰래 그녀와 약혼했다는 (것 말이다).

색 글자 부분은 주어 **rumor**를 수식하는 동격절이다. (a)에서는 뼈대 구조가 쉽게 보이지 않을 뿐만 아니라, 술부(1단어)에 비해 주부(9단어)가 지나치게 길어서, 마치 하체에 비해 머리가 지나치게 큰 아이처럼 불안감을 주므로, 영어는 (b) 구조를 더 좋아한다.

❸

(a) Lincoln appointed men whom he considered most capable for the job **to his cabinet.** (clumsy)

→ (b) Lincoln appointed men **to his cabinet** / whom he considered most capable for the job. (improved)

(a) 링컨은 자기가 생각하기에 그 직책에 가장 유능한 사람들을 자기 내각에 임명했다. (어색함)

(b) 링컨은 사람들을 자기 내각에 임명했다, 자기가 생각하기에 그 직책에 가장 유능한 사람들을 말이다. (더 나음)

밑줄 친 부분은 목적어 men을 수식하는 관계사절이다.

(a)에서는 to his cabinet이 어떤 말과 연관되는지는 쉽게 알 수 없다.

By fighting you never get enough,
but by yielding you get more than you expected.

- Francis Bacon

4. 뼈대구조 먼저 제시 ②

_ 짧은 요소는 앞으로, 긴 요소는 뒤로 이동시킨다

4.1 주부와 보어의 자리 바꿈

❶

(a) The man who, having nothing to say, abstains from giving wordy evidence of the fact, is blessed. (clumsy)

→ (b) Blessed is the man / who, having nothing to say, abstains from giving wordy evidence of the fact. (improved)

(a) 할 말이 없을 때에, 입을 열어 장황하게 그렇다는 증거를 보여주려고 하지 않는 사람은 복을 받는다.
(b) 이런 사람은 복을 받는다, 할 말이 없을 때에 입을 열어 장황하게 그렇다는 증거를 보여주려고 하지 않는 사람 말이다.

🖼 구문

having nothing to say (분사구)
= when he has nothing to say (부사절)

👍 표현

abstains from giving wordy evidence of the fact
= abstains from giving wordy evidence / that he has nothing to say
= does not talk for a long time to show that he has nothing to say
= does not talk
= keeps silent

note abstain from -ing (~하는 것을 삼가다 →) ~하는 것을 아니하다

4.2 목적어와 보어의 자리 바꿈

②

(a) Language makes the exchange of ideas between people possible. (clumsy)

→ (b) Language makes possible the exchange of ideas between people. (improved)

언어는 사람들 사이의 의사 교환을 가능하게 만든다.

(b)에서는 possible까지만 읽으면 그 뒤에 목적어가 나오는 문장의 구조라는 것을 알 수 있다. 그러나 (a)에서는 끝까지 읽어야 그것을 알 수 있으며, 목적어가 매우 긴 경우에는 possible의 역할이 무엇인지 쉽게 파악하지 못할 가능성이 있다.

4.3 목적어와 부사구의 자리 바꿈

③

(a) I will see it to completion. (대명사가 목적어인 경우)

(b) He is reluctant to take on and see to completion any work that will take more than a few weeks or even a few days.

(긴 명사구가 목적어인 경우)

(a) 내가 그것을 끝마치겠다.
(b) 그는 무슨 일이든지 떠맡아서 끝마치기를 싫어한다. 몇 주일 또는 심지어 며칠 이상 걸릴 일은 말이다.

note see to completion: to complete; finish 완성하다: 끝마치다 │ reluctant: unwilling; loath 하고 싶어하지 않는; 싫어하는 │ take on: to undertake; take upon oneself; start on 떠맡다: 착수하다

만일 (b)에서 전치사구 to completion과 그 뒤에 나오는 목적어(any work ... a few days)의 자리를 서로 바꾼다면 — 즉, (a)의 어순을 취한다면 — to completion이라는 말이 어떤 말과 연관되는지 쉽게 알 수 없을 것이다.

5. 뼈대구조 먼저 제시 ③

_예비주어나 예비목적어 'it' 을 사용한다

1
(a) I found to learn English easy. (×)
(b) I found it easy / to learn English. (○)

> **cf** (a) I found (that) to learn English was easy. (○)
> (b) I found (that) it was easy to learn English. (○)

2
(a) I make not to eat between meals a rule. (×)
(b) I make it a rule / not to eat between meals. (○)

나는 원칙적으로 간식을 하지 않는다.

주의
'S+V+O+C' 구문에서 동사는 부정사구를 목적어로 취하지 않는다.

3
(a) I take that you don't want to go with us. (×)
(b) I take it / that you don't want to go with us. (○)

나는 네가 우리와 함께 가기를 원치 않는 것으로 이해하고 있다.

4
(a) Reports have that the prisoner has escaped. (×)
(b) Reports have it / that the prisoner has escaped. (○)

보도에 의하면 그 죄수는 달아났다고 한다.

= It is reported that the prisoner has escaped.
= According to reports, the prisoner has escaped.
= The prisoner has reportedly escaped.

주의

have, take와 같은 일부 타동사는 'that'-clauses를 목적어로 취하지 않는다.

⑤
(a) See to that nobody touches this. (×)
(b) See to it / that nobody touches this. (○)

아무도 이것에 손대지 않도록 해라.

주의

but, except, save를 제외한 일반 전치사는 'that'-clauses를 목적어로 취하지 않는다.

The softest things in the world
overcome the hardest things in the world.

- Lao-tzu

EXERCISE
순해순역 연습

---

1. One of the arguments in favor of birth control is that only those children come into the world / who are genuinely wanted.

---

note   argument 주장 | in favor of: supporting; for 지지하는; 찬성하는 ≠ against 반대하는 | birth control 산아 제한 | come into the world = to be born 태어나다 | genuinely: really; truly 정말로; 진실로

 구문

only those children / who are genuinely wanted / come into the world (이동 전 구조)

---

2. The earthquake shook down in San Francisco hundreds of thousands of dollars' worth of houses and buildings. Not in the history has a modern city been so completely destroyed. Nothing remains / of the city but memories.

---

note   hundreds of thousands (수천의 수백 →) 수십만 | destroy 파괴하다

문맥

"shook down" 흔들어서 쓰러뜨렸다 = "destroyed"

비교

(a) Not in the history has a modern city been so completely destroyed. (강조 어순)

(b) A modern city has not been so completely destroyed in the history. (기본 어순)

전자 (a)에서는 강조받는 부사구가 문두에 옴으로써 주어 city와 조동사 has가 도치된 점에 주의하라.

 구문

Nothing / but memories of the city / remains. 〔이동 전 구조〕

2.1 Stories surfaced / of clashes between director Robert Benton and his star, Dustin Hoffman.

---

3. We must use time creatively, and forever realize that the time is always ripe / to do right. Now is the time to make real the promise of democracy.

`note` creatively 창조적으로 | forever: always 언제나 | realize: to become aware 깨닫다 | ripe: ready 준비되어 있는 | do right 옳은 일을 하다 | make real = to realize 실현하다: 실천하다

 구문

(a) the time is always ripe / to do right 〔이동 후〕
(b) the time / to do right / is always ripe 〔이동 전〕

 연구

영어 동사 표현의 유형

1. (a) be real = be a reality 현실이다 〔상태 표현〕
   (b) become real = become a reality; be realized 실현되다 〔자동 표현〕
   (c) make ~ real = make ~ a reality 실현하다 〔타동 표현〕

2. (a) be known 알려져 있다
   (b) become known 알려지다
   (c) make ~ known 알려지게 만들다

---

4. X-rays are able to pass through objects and thus make visible details / that are otherwise impossible to observe.

---

note pass through 통과하다 | object 물체 | thus: consequently; therefore 그 결과로: 그러므로 | visible: that can be seen 눈으로 볼 수 있는 | detail: a small part 작은 부분 | observe: to see 보다

문맥

"otherwise": in other ways 다른 방법으로 = X-ray를 이용하지 않고
"impossible to observe" = not visible = invisible 눈으로 볼 수 없는

---

5. Libraries make available — through books and a variety of other media — knowledge / that has been accumulated through the ages.

note available: that can be used 이용할 수 있는 | a variety of = various 다양한: 여러 가지의 | media: *pl.* of medium 매체 | accumulate: to gather: collect 모으다: 축적하다 | through the ages 여러 시대에 걸쳐(=역사를 통해)

---

6. We are apt to call barbarous whatever departs widely from our own taste and apprehension.

note be apt to (do): to tend to (do) ~하는 경향이 있다 | barbarous: uncivilized; savage 미개한: 야만적인 | depart: to deviate 벗어나다 | taste 취향 | apprehension: a view; opinion 견해

---

7. We call dangerous those whose minds are constituted differently from ours, and immoral those who do not accept our own morality.

note dangerous: not safe; perilous 위험한 | mind: a way of thinking and feeling; disposition 사고방식 및 감정: 심정 | constitute: to make up; compose 구성하다 | immoral: morally wrong 부도덕한 | morality: a set of rules or principles of conduct 행동 규범 또는 원칙

whose minds are constituted differently from ours
= whose ways of thinking and feeling are different from ours
= who think and feel in different ways from ours

8. The only way in which social life can continue is for each individual to keep unimpaired his or her own independence and self-respect as well as that of others.

note individual 개인 | unimpaired: not impaired; not damaged 손상을 입지 않은; 온전한 〈 impair 손상하다 | independence 독립 | self-respect 자존심 | as well as: in addition to ~뿐만 아니라

9. Astronomers no longer regard as fanciful the idea / that they may some day pick up signals which have been sent by intelligent beings on other worlds.

note astronomer 천문학자 〈 astronomy 천문학 | regard A as B: to think of A as B; look upon A as B (A를 B로 간주하다) | fanciful: unreal 비현실적인; 터무니없는 〈 fancy 공상 | pick up: to succeed in hearing or receiving 청취하거나 포착하다 | intelligent 지성을 갖고 있는 | being: a creature 존재

10. In the nineteenth century many people accepted as scientifically valid not only face-reading, or physiognomy, but also head-reading, or phrenology.

note valid: reasonable; true 합당한; 타당한 | face-reading 관상 | head-reading 골상

문맥
"physiognomy" = "face-reading"
"phrenology" = "head-reading"

여기서 접속사 or는 앞에 나온 말을 다른 말로 바꾸어 설명하기 위한 하나의 장치이다.

11. I thought that I ought to reject as downright false all opinions which I could imagine to be in the least degree open to doubt.

reject: to refuse to accept; discard 받아들이지 아니하다: 버리다 | downright: completely 완전히 | false: erroneous; not true 그릇된: 타당하지 않은 | open to doubt: doubtful; uncertain 의심스러운, 불확실한

12. People who practice totemism, the worship of plants, animals, or objects as gods, usually select for worship objects that are important to the community.

worship 숭배 | object: a material thing 물체: 대상 | community: all the people who live in a particular area; society 어떤 특정한 지역에 거주하는 모든 사람들; 사회

순해

select A for worship = select and worship A
A를 선택해서 숭배하다

문맥

"practice totemism" = 'worship plants, animals, or objects as gods'

13. Seeing is an activity not only of our eyes but of the brain, which works as a sort of selecting machine. Out of all the images presented to it, it chooses for recognition those that fit most neatly with the world learned by past experience.

note sort: a kind 종류 | present: to give 주다 | recognition 인식 〈 recognize 인식하다 | fit 어울리다 | neatly: nicely 잘

 문맥

'choose' = 'select'
"the world" = "those" = "the images"

---

14. Fundamental to the existence of science is a body of established facts which come either from observation of nature in the raw, so to speak, or from experiment.

---

note fundamental: essential; central 근본을 이루는; 핵심적인 | existence 존재 | body: amount; quantity 분량 | establish 확립하다 | fact: an item of knowledge 한 가지 지식 | observation 관찰 | nature in the raw = nature as it is 있는 그대로의 자연 | so to speak: as it were 말하자면 | experiment 실험

구문

C+V+S ('S+V+C' 의 변형)
Complement : Fundamental
Verb : is
Subject : body

---

15. It would be ungrateful not to recognize how immense are the boons which science has given to mankind.

= It would be ungrateful if we did not recognize ...

note ungrateful 배은망덕한 | recognize: to acknowledge 인정하다 | immense: huge; vast 막대한 | boon: a benefit 혜택 | mankind 인류

16. Every year more than 6,000 people die and 130,000 are injured in home fires. Many of these casualties are among the nation's most precious resources, our children. Even more troubling is the fact that many of these deaths could have been prevented had the smoke detectors been operating.

injure: to hurt; wound 다치게 하다 | casualty: a person injured or killed in an accident or disaster 사고나 재난의 사상자 | precious: very valuable 귀중한 | resources 자원 | troubling: distressing 괴로움을 주는 | prevent 막다: 예방하다 | smoke detector 연기 감지기 〈 detect: to sense 감지하다 | operate: to work 작동하다

주의

our children이라는 말로 보아 the nation's에서 the nation은 '그 나라'가 아니라 '우리나라'를 의미한다.

구문

had the smoke detectors been operating

= if the smoke detectors had been operating

가정법 조건절에서 접속사 if를 생략하면 이 절의 주어와 조동사가 서로 자리를 바꾼다.

17. Now at last we have it in our power / to free mankind once and for all from the fear which is based on want.

free: to liberate 해방시키다 | once (and) for all: finally; conclusively 최종적으로 | be based on ~에 기초를 두고 있다 | want: poverty 빈곤

18. They do not believe that they have it in them / to be what they want to be, and so they try to make themselves content with something less than that of which they are capable.

 연구

(1) Mother has made me what I am today.
어머니께서 나를 오늘의 나로 만들어주셨다.
(2) You can be anything (that) you want to be.
= You can be what you want to be.
여러분은 여러분이 되고 싶은 사람이 될 수 있다.
(3) He is no longer what he used to be.
그는 이미 과거의 그가 아니다. = 그는 이제 과거와는 다른 사람이다.

19. He made a great deal of money, but he could never learn to fit expenditure to income, and could never find it in his heart / to resist the cry of another person's distress.

20. John Dickens and his wife were often foolish. They could not get it into their heads / that if you owed money, you had to pay it.

21. Some people take it for granted / that, because science is affecting our lives more and more, it follows / that the scientists themselves are in effective control of the mechanism of civilization and / that in consequence they are immediately and largely responsible for the evils and disasters of our time.

note take ~ for granted ~을 당연한 것으로 여기다 | affect: to have an effect on ~에 영향을 끼치다 | it follows that 따라서 ~라는 결론이 나오다 | be in control of ~을 장악하고 있다 | in consequence: consequently; therefore 그 결과로: 그러므로 | immediate 직접적인 | evil 악 | disaster: a calamity; catastrophe 재난

....

Abilities wither under criticism,
they blossom under encouragement.

- Dale Carnegie

....

6. 뼈대정보 먼저 제시 ①

_ 범주를 먼저 제시한 뒤에 특징이나 세부사항을 얘기한다

이것은 그림을 그릴 때에 윤곽(the outline)을 그리고 나서 세부사항(the details)을 그려넣는 것과 비슷하다.

1
A hedonist is a person / for whom pleasure is the greatest
    the topic   the category   the characteristic

good.

화제   쾌락주의자(는)
범주   사람(인데)
특징   그에게는 쾌락이 최대의 선이다

2
A friendship relationship is one / marked by very close association, contact, or familiarity.

화제   친구 관계
범주   하나의 관계
특징   매우 가까운 교제, 접촉, 또는 친밀

🗨 구문

marked by ... 〔단축 관계사절〕
= which / that is marked by ... 〔관계사절〕

note   marked by = characterized by ~을 특징으로 하는

3 Inflation is an economic condition / in which prices for consumer goods increase, and the value of money or purchasing power decreases.

화제   인플레이션
범주   경제의 상태
특징   이 상태에서는 소비재 가격은 올라가고 화폐 가치 또는 구매력은 떨어진다.

note consumer goods 소비재(소비자 상품) ｜ purchasing power 구매력

4 A computer is a system of electromechanical devices / that receives data, processes this data arithmetically or logically, and then makes this information available to the user.

화제   컴퓨터
범주   전기 기계 장치
특징   자료를 받아서, 산술적으로 또는 논리적으로 처리해서, 이 정보를 사용자가 이용할 수 있게 만들어준다.

note device 장치 〈 devise 고안하다 ｜ process 처리하다 ｜ available: ready for use; usable

Worry is the interest paid on trouble before it falls due.

7. 뼈대정보 먼저 제시 ②

_ 전체에 관한 정보를 먼저 제시하고 나서 부분에 관한 얘기를 한다

① All music has an expressive power, some more and some less.

전체 정보 | 부분 정보

전체 모든 음악은 표현력을 갖고 있다
부분 어떤 것은 더 많이, 어떤 것은 더 적게

② Bats are surprisingly long-lived creatures, some having a life expectancy of around twenty years.

전체 박쥐는 놀라울 정도로 오래 사는 동물이다
부분 일부가 갖고 있는 평균 수명은 약 20년이다

note creature = an animal 동물 ∣ life expectancy (기대 수명 →) 평균 수명

📖 표현
long-lived creatures
= creatures that live long

③ Seventy-three people have been drowned in this area, many of them children.

전체 73명의 사람들이 (지금까지) 이 지역에서 익사했다
부분 이들 중 다수가 어린이들이었다

90

4 The Navy is operating 1,005 ships, 411 of them combatant types.

전체 해군은 1,005척의 배를 운행하고 있다
부분 이 가운데 411척은 '전투형' (전함)이다

note combatant: trained, equipped, and ready for fighting 전투를 위해 훈련받고, 장비가 갖추어져 있으며, 준비되어 있는

5 The earth consists of a number of layers, each with its own kind of solid or liquid matter.

전체 지구는 여러 개의 층으로 이루어져 있다
부분 각 층은 독특한 종류의 고체 또는 액체 물질로 이루어져 있다

note consist of: to be composed of ~로 이루어져 있다 | layer 층 | solid 고체(의) | liquid 액체(의)

Winners never quit and quitters never win.

8. 뼈대정보 먼저 제시 ③

_ 영어의 기본 서술 구조: '핵심어 + 설명(또는 수식)'

1
An orphan is a **child**
whose parents are dead.

핵심 고아는 **아이**다
수식 자기 부모가 죽은
구성 주절 + 관계사절

2
The prisoner lived in a **cell**
measuring about 10 feet long and five feet wide.

핵심 그 죄수는 **감방**에서 살았다
수식 대략 길이가 10피트 그리고 너비가 5피트 나가는
구성 주절 + 단축 관계사절(=분사구)

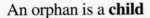 **구문**

measuring about 10 feet long and five feet wide 〔단축 관계사절〕
= that measured ... 〔관계사절〕

3
This is the **ideal**
reflected in the **education**
France provides for her children.

핵심   이것이 그 **이상**이다
수식   그 **교육**에 반영되어 있는
수식   프랑스가 자기 어린이들을 위해 제공하는
구성   주절+단축 관계사절+관계사절

📖 구문

reflected in the education ... [단축 관계사절=분사구]
= that is reflected ... [관계사절]

4

Scientists found no **evidence**

to suggest that neutrinos have mass.

핵심   과학자들은 아무런 **증거**를 찾지 못했다
수식   중성 미자가 질량을 갖고 있다는 것을 보여줄
구성   주절+단축 관계사절(=부정사구)

📖 구문

to suggest that ... [단축 관계사절]
= that would suggest ... [관계사절]

note   suggest: to indicate; show 보여주다 | neutrino 중성 미자 *cf.* neutron 중성자 | mass: the quantity of
matter that anything contains 질량

5

He was a high-spirited **child**,

always up to mischief.

핵심   그는 활기찬 **아이**였다
수식   노상 골치아픈 행동을 하는
구성   주절+단축 관계사절(=형용사구)

📖 구문

always up to mischief [단축 관계사절]
= who was always up to mischief [관계사절]

note high-spirited: lively; energetic 활기찬 | up to: doing 하고 있는 | mischief: conduct that causes harm or trouble 해가 되거나 골치 아프게 만드는 행동

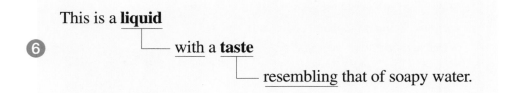

핵심 이것은 **액체**이다
수식 **맛**을 갖고 있는
수식 비눗물의 그것과 비슷한
구성 주절 + 단축 관계사절〔=전치사구〕 + 단축 관계사절〔=분사구〕

 구문

with a taste ... 〔전치사구〕
= that has a taste ... 〔관계사절〕

resembling that of soapy water 〔분사구〕
= that resembles that of soapy water 〔관계사절〕

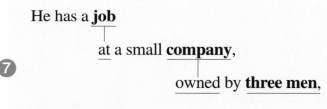

핵심 그는 **일자리**를 갖고 있다
수식 어느 작은 **회사**에
수식 소유주는 **세 사람(남자)**인데
수식 모두 기혼이다
구성 주절 + 전치사구 + 분사구 + 분사구

구문

owned by three men (분사구)
= which is owned by three men (관계사절)

all married (분사구)
= who are all married (관계사절)

Chance is a lady who smiles only upon those few
who know how to make her smile.

9. 뼈대정보 먼저 제시 ④

_ 한국어와 비교 연구

한국어에는 관계사가 없으므로, 모든 영어의 관계사 구문은 한국어와 다르다고 볼 수 있다. 가장 두드러진 차이점은 다음 두 가지인 것 같다.

첫째, 한국어에서는 두 문장(또는 그것에 가까운 구조)으로 나타낼 정보를 영어는 관계사를 이용하여 하나의 문장으로 표현한다.

1
(a) Do not rush into a contract / (that) you are not comfortable with. [전형적인 영어 구조]
(b) Do not rush into a contract / if you are not comfortable with it. [한국어에 가까운 구조]

서둘러 어떤 계약을 체결하지 말아라, 만일 거기에 대해서 안심이 되지 않으면 말이다.

2
(a) He is not a big spender / (that) he once was.
(b) He is not a big spender, / though he once was.

그는 돈을 많이 쓰는 사람이 아니다. 비록 한때는 그랬었지만 말이다.

둘째, 영어에는 기본 문장의 변형으로 만들어진 문장들이 많이 있다. 영어의 구문이 많고 복잡한 이유 가운데 하나가 바로 이런 변형 구조의 발달에 있는 것 같다.

3
(a) An apology is something / (that) she'll never get from me. [변형]
(b) She'll never get an apology from me. [기본]

(a) 사과 같은 것은 결코 그녀가 내게서 받지 못할 것이다. (강조 구문)

(b) 그녀는 결코 내게서 사과를 받지 못할 것이다. (기본 구문)

 구문

(1) It is you that are to blame for the accident. (강조 구문)

(2) You are to blame for the accident. (기본 구문)

너에게 그 사고에 대한 책임이 있다.

❹
(a) This is not something / that would disturb me anyway.
(b) This would not disturb me anyway.

(a) 이와 같은 것은 결코 어떤 방법으로든지 나를 동요시키지 못할 것이다.

(b) 이것은 어떤 방법으로든지 나를 동요시키지 못할 것이다.

note disturb: to upset mentally or emotionally; make uneasy or anxious 마음이나 감정을 뒤흔들어놓다; 동요시키다; 불안하게 만들다 | anyway: in any manner or way 어떤 방법으로든지

Life is not anything; it is only the opportunity for something.

- Christian Friedrich Hebbel

EXERCISE
순해순역 연습

1. (a) A vegetable is a plant, / **such as** cabbage, potato, or onion, / **which** is eaten either raw or cooked.

    (b) Insulin is a substance / (**that** is) produced naturally in the body / **which** controls the level of sugar in the blood.

    (c) A kettle is a covered round container / **with** a handle on the top and a spout on the side, **that** is used for boiling water.

    (d) A table is a piece of furniture / **with** a flat top, / (**which** is) used for putting things on.

note eat raw 날것으로 먹다 (raw=uncooked) | substance 물질 | level 농도 | kettle 주전자 | container 용기 | spout 주둥이 | furniture 가구

2. (a) An ideal is a standard / by which people judge real phenomena. 〈 By the standard of an ideal people judge real phenomena.

    (b) The destination of someone or something is the place / to which they are going or being sent. 〈 They are going or being sent to the place.

    (c) He took two rooms / for which he paid $400 a week. 〈 He paid $400 a week for the two rooms he had taken.

    (d) A seed is the small hard part of a plant / from which a new plant grows. 〈 From a seed a new plant grows.

🧑 **주의**

'전치사＋관계대명사' 구조에서 전치사를 결정해 주는 것은 주로 그 관계대명사의 선행사이거나 그 관계사절의 동사이다.

note **destination** 목적지 ┃ **seed** 씨

👣 **문맥**

"real phenomena" ≠ "an ideal"

note **real phenomena = realities** 현실

---

3. (a) I have a question / I've always wanted to know the answer to. 〈 I've always wanted to know the answer to this question.

(b) Something happened today / I have to tell you about.

(c) I have a problem / I hope you can help me with. 〈 I hope you can be help me with this problem.

(d) Kimchi is the hot pickled cabbage / that no Korean is without. 〈 No Korean is without kimchi.

---

note **pickled** 절인 ┃ **be without = to do without** 없이 지내다

---

4. (a) He can swear like a sailor.

(b) He can swear like the sailor he was.

---

note **swear** 욕하다 ┃ **sailor** 선원

5. (a) America is no longer the melting pot / it once was.

   (b) Economics is not the exact science / that chemistry or biology is.

note melting pot 도가니 | exact: precise; strict 정밀한 | chemistry 화학

6. (a) She was not the cheerful woman / she had been.

   (b) Mitchum was two things / De Niro isn't: big and sexy.

note cheerful: gay; joyful 명랑한

7. (a) He's not in love with me. He's in love with the woman he thinks I am.

   (b) We have to find out if they are really who they claim they are.

note be in love with ~을 사랑하고 있다 | claim 주장하다

8. (a) I have a fairly good understanding of the kind of person I am.

   (b) Listen to someone speak for a few moments, or read something which he has written, and you will learn much about the kind of person he is.

(a) = I understand fairly well what kind of person I am.

(b) = **If** you listen to someone speak for a few moments, or read something which he has written, you will learn much about what kind of person he is.

 구문

Add love to a house **and** you have a home. (명령문)

= If you add love to a house, you have a home.

집에 사랑을 보태면 가정이 된다.

---

9. It is not our public behavior that reveals the sort of fellows we are. It only indicates the kind of fellows we desire the world to take us to be. We want the world's good opinion, and when we go out, we put on our good manners as we put on our best clothes in order to win it.

---

note public behavior=behavior in public 남들이 있을 때에 하는 행동 │ **indicate: to show** 보여주다 │ **take A to be B** A를 B로 받아들이다 │ **opinion: estimation** 평가 │ **put on** 몸에 걸치다; 착용하다 │ **win: to gain** 얻다

 문맥

"indicates" = "reveals"

---

10. No smoker who exercises good manners should be treated like a leper. However, people who light up around strangers, as someone recently did in front of me in the post office, deserve to be treated like the insensitive clods they truly are.

---

note **exercise good manners** 예절 바르게 행동하다 │ **treat** 다루다; 취급하다 │ **leper: an outcast** 버림받은 사람 │ **light up: to smoke** 담배를 피우다 │ **insensitive: uncaring** 남들의 고통에 대해서 신경을 쓰지 않는 │ **clod: a stupid person; idiot** 멍청이; 백치

11. Recently my son had a terrible traffic accident. The doctors told me he would need several reconstructive surgeries and the outcome was something no one could predict.

note traffic accident 교통 사고 | reconstructive surgeries 복원 수술 | outcome: a result 결과 | predict: to foresee 예견하다; 예측하다

12. Your husband's treatment of you is abominable. Why you tolerate such emotional abuse is something that you ought to look into with the help of a counselor.

note abominable: disgusting 가증스러운 | tolerate: to put up with 허용하다; 견디다 | emotional: mental 정신적인 | abuse: cruel and violent treatment 학대 | look into: to investigate; examine 조사하다; 진찰하다

13. Science in this country is still facing several problems, some traditional and some modern.

note face (v.): to be faced with; experience ~에 직면하다; 경험하다 | traditional 전통적인

14. By the age of five, about 87% of American children are attending school, most of them in preacademic classes called kindergarten.

note attend school: to go to school 학교에 다니다 | preacademic = preschool 취학 전의 | kindergarten (어린이 마당 →) 유치원

15. The bomb set off by the Irish Republican Army (IRA) on November 8, 1987, killed 11 and injured 61. All were innocent civilians, the youngest two months old.

note set off: to cause to explode 폭발시키다 〈타동사〉 → go off 폭발하다 〈자동사〉 | IRA 아일랜드 공화국군 | innocent: blameless 아무 죄도 없는 | civilian 민간인

16. (a) He is a wise man **who** wastes no energy on pursuits for which he is not fitted; and he is still wiser **who**, from among the things that he can do well, chooses and resolutely follows the best.

(b) A wise man wastes no energy on pursuits for which he is not fitted; and a still wiser man, from among the things that he can do well, chooses and resolutely follows the best.

note waste A on B A를 B에 낭비하다 | fitted 적합한 | resolutely: determinedly; steadfastly 단호히, 꾸준히

Failures are rehearsals for success.

10. 핵심어에 대한 추가 설명 ①

_ 첨가 정보: '대명사(+수식어구)'

❶ All cultures, even the simplest (one), seem to be in a continuous state of change.

모든 문화는, 가장 **단순한 문화까지도**, 계속적인 변화 상태 속에 있는 것 같다.

표현
be in a continuous state of change = to change continuously
be in favor of = to favor 지지하다
be in agreement with = to agree with ~와 일치하다
be on one's guard against = to guard against ~에 대해서 경계하다
be on the rise = to be rising 오르고 있다

❷ Life is potentially meaningful under any conditions, even those which are most miserable.

인생은 어떤 상태 하에서도, **가장 비참한 상태에서까지도**, 의미를 가질 수 있다.

> **note** potential: possible 가능한 | miserable: very unhappy 매우 불행한

표현
Life is potentially meaningful.
= **Life can** be meaningful.
= **Life can** have meaning.

❸ A bug is a tiny insect, especially one that causes damage or that people find unpleasant.

벌레는 작은 곤충이다, 특히 해를 끼치거나 사람들에게 불쾌감을 주는 것 말이다.

❹ A pond is a small area of water, smaller than a lake, often one that has been artificially created.

연못은 작은 면적의 수역인데, 호수보다 작으며, 흔히 인위적으로 만든 것이다.

`note` artificial: man-made 인간에 의해 만들어진 ≠ natural | create: to make 만들다

One doesn't recognize in one's life the really important momnets
— until it's too late.

- Agatha Christie

---

11. 핵심어에 대한 추가 설명 ②

_첨가 정보: 'if, though, etc.+x'

❶ There is little hope, if any, for his quick recovery.

이것은 다음 문장이 간소화된 것이다.

There is little hope, if there is any hope, for his quick recovery.
거의 가망이 없다 ─ 설사 있다고 하더라도 ─ 그가 빨리 회복할 가망 말이다.

구문

(a) There is little hope / for his quick recovery. 〔단문〕
(b) There is little hope that he will recover quickly. 〔복문〕

❷ The economy of the country boasts a steady if unspectacular annual growth rate of 3%.

그 나라의 경제는 꾸준한 ─ 비록 대단치 않지만 ─ 연간 3%의 성장률을 자랑한다.

note boast 자랑하다 | unspectacular: not spectacular; modest 대단찮은: 보통 정도의 | annual: yearly 1년 간의

❸ William Blake, who is now considered one of the great though eccentric voices of English Romanticism, was virtually unknown in his own day.

윌리엄 블레이크는 지금은 영국 낭만주의의 위대한 ─ 비록 별나지만 ─ 대표적인 작가들 중의 한 사람으로 간주되지만 그의 당대에는 사실상 무명이었다.

eccentric 원형에서 벗어난: out of the ordinary; not usual 별난 | virtually: actually 실제로

🔥 문맥

"voices" = representative writers 대표하는 작가들

---

4 Such a decision will bring about harmful *if not fatal* results.

그런 결정은 해로운 — 비록 심각한 것은 아니지만 — 결과들을 가져올 것이다.

bring about: to cause to happen 일어나게 하다 (타동 표현) → come about 발생하다 (자동 표현) | fatal: serious; important 심각한; 중대한 〈 fate 운명

There is nothing either good or bad but thinking makes it so.

- William Shakespeare

12. 핵심어에 대한 추가 설명 ③

_ 첨가 정보: 'and + x'

❶ You've been had, and had badly.

넌 속임을 당했다, 그것도 심하게 당했단 말이다.

note have: to deceive; cheat 속이다 | badly: very much 매우 많이

❷ From the distinctive sound of a high-heeled shoes on the marble floor, he knew it was a lady, and probably a slender one at that.

대리석 바닥 위의 또렷한 하이힐 구두 소리로 보아, 그는 그게 여자라는 것을 알았다. **그것도 아마 날씬한 여자이리라는 것을 말이다.**

note distinctive: clear 또렷한 | marble 대리석 | slender: long and thin; slim 날씬한

❸ Atoms, and thus all material substances, **consist largely of empty space.**

원자는 ― 그리고 따라서 모든 물질은 ― 대부분 빈 공간으로 구성되어 있다.

note atom 원자 | thus: therefore 그러므로 | material: physical 물질적인 | substance: matter 물질 | consist of: to be composed of ~로 구성되어 있다 | largely: for the most part; mainly 대부분; 주로

4 If we are not too proud to explain ourselves or to ask explanations of others, most of the misunderstandings of our life would disappear, and many of our worries with them.

만일 우리가 너무 거만하게 굴지 않고 우리의 입장을 설명해 주거나 남들에게 자기들의 입장을 설명해 달라고 하면, 인생의 오해들의 대부분은 사라질 것이다. **그리고 우리의 걱정들 중 다수도 그것들과 함께 말이다.**

🔖 문맥

"ask explanations of others" = ask others to explain themselves

📖 구문

(a) too **proud** to do 너무 거만해서 하지 아니하는
(b) not too **proud** to do 너무 거만하게 굴지 아니하는

Attitudes are more important than facts.

- Karl Menninger

---

1. To be in company, even with the best, is soon wearisome and dissipating. I love to be alone.

> **note** be in company: to be with another person or other people 다른 사람 또는 사람들과 함께 지내다 | wearisome: tiresome; tedious 지치게 하는; 지루한 | dissipating (낭비하는 →) 시간과 정력을 낭비하는

---

2. A blunder is a big mistake, especially one which seems to be the result of carelessness or stupidity.

> **note** careless: not careful; thoughtless 부주의한 | stupid: not wise; foolish 어리석은

---

3. An ailment is an illness, especially one that does not seem serious even though it might be unpleasant or painful and last a long time.

> **note** serious: severe; grave 심한; 중대한 | last (v.): to go on; continue 계속되다

---

4. Human kindness can be found in all groups, even those which as a whole it would be easy to condemn.

note as a whole: altogether 전체적으로 *cf.* on the whole: in general 일반적으로 | condemn: to disapprove of strongly; censure 비난하다

---

5. I have always wondered at the passion many people have to meet the celebrated. The celebrated develop a technique to deal with the persons they come across. They show the world a mask, often an impressive one, but take care to conceal their real selves. They play the part that is expected from them, and with practice learn to play it very well, but you are stupid if you think that this public performance of theirs corresponds with the man within.

---

note wonder at ~에 대해서 감탄하다 | the celebrated (the + 형용사) = celebrated people = celebrities 유명한 사람들 | develop 개발하다 | come across: to meet by chance 우연히 만나다 | conceal: to hide 숨기다 | correspond with ~와 일치하다

 문맥

"public performance" = "mask"

"the man within" = "their real selves"

---

6. Jesus described His mission in this world: "I have come that you might have life and have it in all its fullness."

---

note describe: to tell about ~에 대해서 얘기하다 | mission: duty; purpose 임무; 목적 | in all its fullness 최대한 충실하게

구문

(so) that ~ may ... ~가 …하도록

7. There is only one Henry Moore in this show of modern sculpture, and a very early one at that, a 1929 stone figure.

8. He looked a full twenty years younger than he really was and this without apparent surgical enhancement.

 연구

수식어 첨가에 따른 부정관사의 첨가

1. (a) twenty years
   (b) a full twenty years 꽉 찬 20년
2. (a) Clinton
   (b) an angry Clinton 화난 클린턴

....

Knowledge of what is possible is the beginning of happiness.

- George Santayana

....

13. 핵심어에 대한 추가 설명 ④

_동격어구

1 **Synonyms,** words that have the same basic meaning, **do not always have the same emotional meaning.**

동의어, 즉 같은 기본적 의미를 갖고 있는 단어들이 반드시 같은 감정적 의미를 갖고 있는 것은 아니다.

주의
"Synonyms" = "words that have the same basic meaning"

2 **Black lung,** a condition that develops after years of breathing coal dust, **gradually robs the lungs of their ability to absorb oxygen.**

'검은 폐' 는 수년 동안 탄진을 호흡한 후에 발생하는 상태인데, 점차 폐에게서 산소를 받아들일 능력을 빼앗는다.

note **develop: to occur** 발생하다 | **gradually: little by little** 조금씩: 점차 | **rob A of B** A에게서 B를 빼앗다 | **absorb: to take in** 받아들이다 | **oxygen** 산소

3 **Tears continually bathe the cornea,** the outer layer of the eyeball.

눈물은 계속해서 각막 — 안구의 바깥층 — 을 씻어준다.

note **outer** 바깥쪽의 ≠ **inner** | **layer: a single thickness or fold** 층

4 Americans admire the self-made person – the one who, with neither money nor family influence, fights his or her way to the top.

미국인들은 자수 성가한 사람 — 즉 돈이나 가족의 영향력 없이 노력해서 정상에 오르는 사람 — 을 찬양한다.

note admire: to have high regard for 찬양하다 | self-made 자수 성가한 → self-taught 독학한

 연구

기본 표현과 파생 표현

make one's way 가다 (기본)
find one's way 길을 찾아서 가다 (파생)
walk one's way 걸어서 가다
fight one's way 노력해서 가다
shoot one's way 총을 쏘면서 가다

It all depends on how we look at things,
and not on how they are in themselves.

- Carl Jung

EXERCISE
순해순역 연습

1. Many children feel the same way Hurley once did about books — indifferent.

2. In London, British officials resorted to an Americanism to deny the assertion: "Baloney!"

3. Most cells contain many mitochondria, semi-independent structures that supply the cell with readily usable energy.

4. In all his eighty-seven years my grandfather did not allow his picture to be taken even once. He claimed that the "black box" — the (   ) — would steal his soul.

문제

( ) 안에 적절한 말을 넣으시오.

힌트

picture 사진 → the "black box" 검은 상자 = ?

---

5. The artist gives us new eyes, eyes with which we can see aspects of reality which we did not dream were there.

note aspect: a side 면 | reality 현실 | dream: to imagine 상상하다

---

6. In the distant past, scientists viewed the earth as the center of the universe. One of the earliest documented models of this view was that of Claudius Ptolemy, a Greek astronomer who lived in the second century.

note view: to regard 간주하다 | universe 우주 | documented: recorded 기록된 | astronomer 천문학자

---

7. One convenient way of discovering and following an author's thesis is to look for key words, those that not only appear frequently but also seem charged with more than casual significance.

note convenient: handy 편리한 | thesis: a proposition; argument 주장 | charged: filled 채워져 있는 | casual: incidental 부수적인 | significance: meaning 의미

8. **France might be described as an 'all-round' country,** one that has achieved results of equal importance in many diverse branches of artistic and intellectual activity.

note **describe: to tell about** ~에 대해 얘기하다 | **all-round** 〔영국영어〕, **all-around** 〔미국영어〕: having many abilities or talents 다재 다능한 | **achieve: to gain; attain** 이루다; 획득하다 | **diverse: different** 다른 | **branch: a field; area** 분야

9. **Perseverance,** that all-important "if at first you don't succeed, try, try again" attitude, **is the primary quality in every success story.**

note **perseverance: continued, patient effort; persistence** 끈질긴 노력; 끈기 | **all-important: highly important** 지극히 중요한 | **primary: first in importance** 제일 중요한 | **quality: a characteristic element** 특징적인 요소

10. **A characteristic of American culture that has become almost a tradition is the glorification of the self-made man —** the man who has risen to the top through his own efforts, usually beginning by working with his hands.

note **characteristic: a distinguishing quality** 특징 | **tradition** 전통 | **glorify: to praise** 칭찬하다 | **rise to** ~에 오르다 | **working with his hands = manual labor** 육체 노동

11. Life is very complicated, and it is art's business to simplify it. The artist must find the common denominator, that which is similar among us, and draw upon that to produce a work which not only unites us but also separates us. Each of us must be able to see something different in the work, although the underlying thing we grasp in it is the same.

note complicated: not simple; complex 복잡한 | common denominator 공통 분모 | draw upon: to make use of 이용하다 | underlying: fundamental; basic 근본적인

 문맥
"grasp" = "see"

12. Educators in Japan are alarmed at the rise of "school refusal syndrome" — a psychological ailment of kids too stressed out to face going to class.

note alarm: to make anxious; frighten 불안하게 만들다; 두려워하게 만들다 | psychological: of the mind; mental 마음의; 정신적인 | kid: a child | stressed out (스트레스를 받아 나간 →) 스트레스를 받아 제구실을 못하는 → burned-out 타버려서 제구실을 못하는

 문맥
"syndrome" = "ailment"
"class" = "school"

13. Mary suffers from SAD, short for seasonal affective disorder, a syndrome characterized by severe seasonal mood swings.

short for ~을 줄인 | affective: emotional 정서적인; 감정의 | disorder: a disturbance in physical or mental health 장애 | characterized by ~로 특징지어진 | severe: extreme 심한 | swing: a change 변화

문맥

"syndrome" = "disorder"
"mood" = "affective"

구문

characterized by ... 〔단축 관계사절〕
= that is characterized by ... 〔관계사절〕

---

14. In every language there seem to be certain "unmentionables" — words of such strong suggestion that they cannot be used in polite conversation. In English, the first of these to come to mind are, of course, words dealing with bodily discharge. We ask movie ushers and filling-station attendants where the "lounge" or "rest room" is, although we usually have no intention of lounging or resting.

---

unmentionables (n.): words that are not to be mentioned 입에 담을 수 없는 말들 | suggestion: an implication 암시 | polite: showing good manners 품위 있는 | come to mind 머릿속에 떠오르다 | deal with ~을 다루다 | bodily discharge 신체의 배설 | usher 좌석 안내원("어서" 오세요!) | filling station 주유소 | attendant 종업원

구문

dealing with ... 〔단축 관계사절〕
= that deal with ... 〔관계사절〕

연구

하이픈의 기능

1. (a) filling station 〔명사〕
   (b) filling-station 〔형용사〕
2. (a) middle class 〔명사〕
   (b) middle-class 〔형용사〕

15. The best-known and most controversial technique used by biotechnology is gene-splicing, the insertion of foreign genes into plants, animals or microbes. Scientists have, for example, introduced rat-growth-hormone genes into the DNA of mice, resulting in larger mice, and firefly genes into tobacco plants, which then glow in the dark. Genetic engineering cannot, however, "cross" a cow with a frog to produce a new species.

note controversial 논란의 대상인 | biotechnology 생물 공학 | gene-splicing 유전자 결합 | mice: plural of mouse 생쥐 | firefly 개똥벌레 | tobacco 담배 | glow: to give off light without heat; shine 빛을 내다: 반짝이다 | insertion 삽입 | foreign gene 다른 생물의 유전자 | microbe 미생물 | genetic engineering 유전 공학 | cross 교배시키다 | species 종

문맥

"introduce" = 'insert'
"produce" = 'result in'
"genetic engineering" = "gene-splicing"

구문

resulting in ... (단축 관계사절)
= which resulted in ... (관계사절)

16. Scientists are increasingly convinced that the burning of fossil fuels is contributing to the greenhouse effect, a potentially dangerous warming of the globe caused by carbon dioxide and other exhaust gases. Unless the growth of fuel consumption is slowed dramatically or nonfossil energy sources, including solar and nuclear, are expanded rapidly, the world could face climatic changes leading to widespread flooding and famine.

구문

caused by ... (단축 관계사절)
= that is caused by ... (관계사절)

leading to ... (단축 관계사절)
= that could lead to ... (관계사절)

If someone else can make you happy and unhappy,
you are not a master. You are just a slave...
Only a MASTER of oneself can transcend anguish.

- B. S. Rajneesh

14. 핵심어에 대한 추가 설명 ⑤

_ 환언 설명

같은 내용을 달리 설명한 말을 필자는 환언 설명이라고 부른다. 이것이 동격어구와 다른 점은 여기에는 일반적으로 이것이 환언 설명이라는 것을 보여주기 위한 말들(환언 설명 장치들)이 그 설명 앞에 나온다는 점이다.

❶ There are two forms **or** aspects of science.

과학에는 두 가지 형태 또는 양상이 있다.

주의
"aspects" = "forms"
환언 설명 장치: or

❷ You can read the story in the first book of the Bible, **namely**, Genesis.

우리는 그 이야기를 성경의 첫 번째 책, 즉, 창세기에서 읽을 수 있다.

주의
"Genesis" = "the first book of the Bible"
환언 설명 장치: namely

❸ Does he ever date? **I mean** — go out with girls?

도대체 그가 데이트하는 적이 있느냐? 내 말은 — 여자들과 밖에 나가느냐는 말이다.

주의

"go out with girls" = "date"

환언 설명 장치: I mean

④ The number of miners killed in accidents each year is between 60 and 70, about half the annual toll of a decade ago.

매년 사고로 사망하는 광부의 수는 60명과 70명 사이인데, 이것은 10년 전 연간 사망자 수의 약 절반이다.

"about half the annual toll of a decade ago" = "between 60 and 70"

문맥

"the annual toll" = "the number of miners killed in accidents each year"

가장 많이 사용되는 환언 설명 장치들은 다음과 같다.

comma, or, that is (to say), i.e., in other words, etc.

You don't have a problem to solve.
You just have a decision to make.

- Robert H. Schuller

EXERCISE
순해순역 연습

1. You should have consulted an ophthalmologist, that is, an eye doctor.

 문제

ophthalmologist는 무엇인가?

2. A topic sentence is a complete sentence; that is, it contains a subject and a verb.

topic sentence : 한 문단의 중심이 되는 문장으로, 주제(the main idea)를 밝혀주며, 대개 문단의 첫머리에 온다.

3. Every good paragraph has unity, which means that in each paragraph, only one main idea is discussed.

note　unity 통일성 ∣ discuss: to talk or write about ~에 대해서 논하다

4. Surveys show that 17 million to 22 million, or 7% to 9%, of adult Americans are functionally illiterate, vs. less than 1% of Japanese.

note survey 조사 | adult: grown-up 성인이 된 | functionally illiterate (기능적으로 문맹인 →) 사회 생활에 필요한 글을 읽고 쓸 줄 모르는 vs. (an abbreviation for 'versus'): as compared to('versus'의 약자) ~에 비해서

5. In 1953 James Watson and Francis Crick unveiled the structure of deoxyribonucleic acid, or DNA, the material from which genes are made.

note unveil: to disclose; reveal 밝히다 | gene 유전자

6. Aristotle, the Greek philosopher, summed up the four chief qualities of money some 2,000 years ago. It must be lasting and easy to recognize, to divide, and to carry about. In other words, it must be durable, distinct, divisible, and (p   ).

 문제

(   ) 안에 들어갈 가장 알맞은 단어를 쓰시오(p로 시작할 것).

힌트

"durable" = "lasting" 오래가는
"distinct" = "easy to recognize" 알아보기 쉬운
"divisible" = "easy to divide" 나누기 쉬운
"p_____" = "easy to carry about" 이리저리 가지고 다니기 쉬운

7. Culture is essentially a product of leisure. From the Chinese point of view, the man who is wisely _____ is the most cultured man.

📖 문제
빈칸에 가장 알맞은 말은?

① idle   ② learned
③ busy   ④ able

🔍 힌트
주어진 구절은 '교양'과 '여가'의 관계를 다루고 있다.

note essentially: in essence; basically 본질적으로; 근본적으로 | point of view 관점

🖊 요령
교양은 여가의 산물이다. (그러므로) _____인 사람이 가장 교양 있는 사람이다. 따라서 빈 칸에는 '여가'와 관계 있는 말이 와야 한다.

💡 문맥
"idle" = having leisure

8. Ideas can sometimes be communicated better by gestures than by words. It is much less effective to tell a person to leave the room than to _____ .

📖 문제
빈칸에 가장 알맞은 말은?

① ask him to go   ② say nothing at all
③ point to the door   ④ get up and go out

손짓이 말보다 때로는 더 효과적이다.

---

9. Both content and style are essential to good poetry. A good subject alone does not insure a good poem, and an elaborate form is ridiculous in the absence of _____ .

문제

빈칸에 가장 알맞은 말은?

① something to say   ② a complex purpose
③ elaborate style   ④ insignificant content

힌트

둘째 문장은 첫째 문장에 대한 환언 설명이라고 볼 수 있다.

note content 내용 | essential: absolutely necessary 절대로 필요한 | insure: to guarantee 보장하다 | ridiculous: ludicrous 우스운 | in the absence of: without 없으면

문맥

"content" = "subject" = "something to say"
"style" = "form"
"elaborate" = "good"
"an elaborate form is ridiculous in the absence of something to say"
= a good form alone does not insure a good poem, either.

---

10. If we are to improve the quality of a piece of writing, we must do more than merely criticize it. We must explain why we criticize it. Inferior work is most effectively remedied when we know _____ .

문제

빈칸에 가장 알맞은 말은?

① who wrote it   ② why it is poor

③ exactly how poor it is   ④ what good writing it is

 문맥

"do more than merely criticize it" = "explain why we criticize it"
"work" = "piece of writing"
"remedied" = "improved"
"why it is poor" = "why we criticize it"
"poor" = "inferior"

---

11. To be happy, a man must feel, firstly, free, and, secondly, important. He cannot be really happy if he is compelled by society to do what he does not enjoy doing, or if what he enjoys doing is ignored by society as of no value or importance.

note   compel: to force 강요하다 | ignore A as B A를 B라는 이유로 무시하다

🖊 주제

행복의 두 가지 조건: 자유와 중요성(가치)

---

12. The examples below demonstrate two different types of concluding sentences of a paragraph. The first one paraphrases the topic sentence; i.e., the concluding sentence repeats the main idea of the topic sentence in different words. The second example summarizes the main points of the paragraph, which were not specifically stated in the topic sentence.

문제

문단의 종결 문장의 두 유형을 간단히 설명하라.

demonstrate: to show; illustrate 보여주다: 예시하다 │ summarize: to sum up 요약하다 │ specifically: definitely 구체적으로 │ state: to set forth in words 밝히다

*Old age occurs the moment you realize
there isn't something wonderful
about to happen just around the corner.*

- D. E. Short

15. 핵심어에 대한 추가 설명 ⑥

_부연 설명

앞에 나온 말의 일부 또는 전부를 명사나 대명사로 받아서 그것을 설명해 주는 말을
필자는 부연 설명(문법학자들은 이것을 동격구로 취급함)이라고 부른다. 구조적으로
볼 때, 부연 설명의 뼈대는 '명사(또는 대명사)＋수식어구' 로 이루어져 있다.

❶ The pre-Incan Nasca Indians sculpted fantastic figures of
birds and animals in the sand, figures so huge that they can be
seen only from the air.

잉카 이전의 나스카 인디언들은 새와 동물들의 믿을 수 없을 만큼 큰 형상들을 모래에 만들었는데, 이 형상들은 너무도
거대해서 공중에서만 볼 수 있다.

부연 설명: "figures so huge ... from the air"

note sculpt: to make 만들다 → sculpture 조각 | huge: very large; gigantic 거대한

📖 문맥
"fantastic" = "huge"

❷ Suddenly he feels free — the freedom that rises out of total
dispair.

갑자기 그는 자유를 느낀다 — 완전한 절망에서 일어나는 그런 자유 말이다.

note total: complete 완전한

130

3 Great thinkers have lamented man's loneliness in this world. Now comes another voice, one that is far more stronger than all the previous ones.

위대한 사상가들은 이 세상에서의 인간의 고독을 슬퍼해 왔다. 이제 또 한 사람이 그런 소리를 하는데, 그의 목소리는 모든 종전의 그것들보다 훨씬 더 강하다.

note lament: to feel or express deep sorrow for ~에 대해서 슬퍼하다

4 He was practical always — something (that) he learned growing up on a farm.

그는 언제나 실제적이었는데 — 이 점은 그가 농장에서 성장하면서 익힌 것이었다.

5 His memory on little things blanked out, a sign of aging.

= His memory on little things blanked out, a sign that he was aging.
= His memory on little things blanked out, which was a sign of aging.
작은 일에 대한 그의 기억은 희미해졌는데, 이것은 그가 늙어가고 있다는 징조였다.

🔎 관찰
이런 부연 설명 어구는 'which'-clauses가 줄어들어서 이루어진 것이라고 볼 수 있다.

note blank out: to become obscured or blotted out 희미해지거나 지워지다 | age: to grow old 늙어가다

6 The scientists wanted their research to be useful, an indication of their desire to work for the benefit of humanity.

= The scientists wanted their research to be useful, an indication that they desired to work for the benefit of humanity.

= ..., which was an indication that ...

= ..., which indicated that ...

그 과학자들은 자기들의 연구가 쓸모가 있기를 바랐는데, 이것은 그들이 인류의 혜택을 위해 일하고 싶어한다는 증거였다.

비교

5, 6번 예문과 같은 앞부분 전체에 대한 부연 설명은 다음과 같은 'which'-clauses와 비슷한 점을 갖고 있다.

(1) He likes dogs, which surprises me.

그는 개를 좋아하는데, 그것이 나를 놀라게 한다.

(2) He arrived half an hour late, which annoyed us all very much.

그는 반 시간 늦게 도착했는데, 그것이 우리 모두를 무척 짜증나게 했다.

note annoy: to irritate; make a little angry 짜증나게 하다; 다소 화나게 만들다

Every day is a new life to a wise man.
Think that this day will never dawn again.

- Dante

EXERCISE
순해순역 연습

---

1. Gamblers Anonymous taught me how to stop gambling, something I had long tried to do by myself without success.

> **note** Gamblers Anonymous 도박 중독자들을 돕기 위한 도박 중독자 단체 → Alcoholics Anonymous | by oneself: through one's own efforts; unaided 자신의 노력을 통해서; 남의 도움을 받지 않고

---

2. Teachers usually spend many hours correcting papers, a task that few of them enjoy.

> **note** spend A (in) ~ing A를 소비해서 ~하다 | correct (v.) 고치다 | paper: a short essay, especially one written as an assignment in a school course 짧은 글, 특히 학교 강좌에서 숙제로 쓴 것

---

3. Norman may be pretending to be sick to avoid going to school, a possibility that we cannot ignore.

> **note** pretend 체하다 | ignore: to disregard 무시하다

---

4. Jane Goodall discovered that chimpanzees in the wild make and use tools — signs of intelligence long thought to be restricted to man.

the wild: the nature; natural habitat 자연; 자연 서식지 | restricted: confined; limited 한정된; 제한된

 구문

long thought to be restricted to man [단축 관계사절]
= that has long been thought to be restricted to man [관계사절]

---

5. Economic growth could provide the resources for better education and more effective health care — areas where the public sector must play the primary role.

---

resources 자원 → natural resources 천연 자원 | effective 효과적인 | health care 건강 관리 | public sector 경제의 공공 부문 ≠ private sector | primary: first in importance 제일 중요한

---

6. The Korean War gave China great opportunity ... to get Russia out of North Korea — an aspect of that climacteric conflict which we in the West all too easily overlooked.

---

great: very good 아주 좋은 | aspect: a side or part 측면 또는 부분 | climacteric: crucial; critical 매우 중대한; 결정적인 | conflict: war 전쟁 | all too: very 아주 | overlook: to ignore 무시하다

 문맥

"that climacteric conflict" = "the Korean War"

---

7. When he shook hands with me, he looked away, a trait I put down to shyness.

= When he shook hands with me, he looked away, which I put down to shyness.

134

note trait: a distinguishing characteristic or quality 특징 | put A down to B = to attribute A to B A가 B에 기인한다고 생각하다 | shy 수줍어하는

8. Berica inherited her father Dino's sharp mind and iron resolve — qualities he'd used to become one of the most successful Venetian businessmen.

note inherit ~을 물려받다 〈 heir 상속인 | sharp mind 예리한 두뇌 | iron resolve: firm resolution 굳은 결심

9. In a television address, the President pleaded for "patience" — a virtue in ever shorter supply as businesses fail and unemployment lines grow longer.

note address: a speech, especially a formal one 연설 | plead: to make an earnest appeal 충심으로 호소하다 | virtue 덕목 | unemployment 실업

10. I have a 5-year-old daughter who is blind. She is constantly confronted with pity — a reaction she does not understand. Strangers come up to her saying, "Oh, bless your heart. You poor little thing."

note blind 눈 먼 | constantly: always 노상 | be confronted with: to be faced with ~와 부딪치다 | pity 동정 | reaction: a response 반응 | come up: to come near; approach 다가오다 | bless: to protect from evil 악으로부터 보호하다

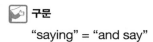 구문

"saying" = "and say"

11. The trading firm is a whopping $2.6 billion in debt, an amount that dwarfs the value of its assets.

note trading firm 무역 회사 │ whopping: extraordinarily large or great 엄청나게 많거나 큰 │ dwarf ~보다 훨씬 더 커서 ~을 아주 작아 보이게 만들다 │ assets 자산 ≠ liabilities 부채

문법

(a) five dollars
(b) a mere five dollars 불과 5달러

12. He is the father of human-powered flight, the inventor of airplanes with propellers driven solely by the pilot's leg muscles — a feat mankind had dreamed of for thousands of years but always failed to accomplish, until MacCready came along. (He = MacCready)

note human-powered flight 사람의 힘을 동력으로 하는 비행 │ drive: to set in motion; supply power for 작동시키다; ~을 위한 동력을 제공하다 │ solely: only 오로지 │ muscle 근육 │ feat: a noteworthy or extraordinary achievement 주목할 만하거나 놀라운 업적 │ accomplish: to achieve 성취하다 │ come along: to appear 나타나다

13. Why do many women work outside the home? One reason is that their jobs bring them genuine satisfaction. A recent survey indicates that the number of women attending colleges is increasing more and more. Women want to make creative use of the skills they acquire and the interests they develop as a result of their education — skills and interests there is often little opportunity to use in keeping house. Another reason is financial. Two incomes in a family are often necessary if a husband and wife would like to maintain a standard of living.

note genuine: real 진정한 | satisfaction 만족 〈 satisfy (v.) | recent 최근의 | survey 조사 | indicate: to show 보여주다 | attend ~에 다니다 | more and more 점점 더 많이 | make use of = to use 이용하다 | acquire: to get 얻다 | develop: to get; acquire 획득하다 | keep house 가사에 종사하다 | financial: having to do with money matters; economic 금전적인; 경제적인 | income 수입: 소득 | maintain: to keep up 유지하다 | standard of living 생활 수준

 구문

attending colleges (단축 관계사절)
= who attend colleges (관계사절)

---

14. A biosensor can immediately measure the amount of poison in the body, a process that now takes several hours. It can exactly monitor glucose levels in a diabetic's blood 24 hours a day to determine when insulin is needed, a process now based on rough estimates.

note immediately: at once; instantly 즉각: 순식간에 | poison 독물: 독약 | monitor 점검하다 | glucose 포도당 | diabetic 당뇨병 환자 〈 diabetes 당뇨병 | determine: to find out 알아내다 | based on ~에 기초를 둔 | rough estimate 어림셈

---

15. But size and price cannot explain why computers have taken such a strong hold on so many youngsters. Many experts, and most of the young operators, agree that the overwhelming attraction is the lure of control, the pleasure of being able to think out and then make something happen — a satisfaction all too often denied children.

note take hold on 사로잡다 | youngster: a child | expert: a specialist 전문가 | operator = a user 사용자 | overwhelming 압도적인 | attraction 매력 | lure = attraction 유혹 | think out 생각해내다

16. According to one national survey completed in 1985, primary-school classes spent only seven or eight minutes each day actually reading. The rest of their lessons were spent completing worksheets or answering multiple-choice questions — not activities designed to stimulate interest in reading. Under the new system, students will read for longer stretches and then discuss the stories in class.

note national: nationwide 전국적인 | survey 조사 | primary-school (adj.) 초등학교의 〈 primary school 초등학교 | worksheet 연습문제지 | multiple-choice 선다형의 | designed to (do) (하도록) 의도된: (하는) 것을 목적으로 하는 | stimulate 자극하다 〈 stimulus 자극 | stretch (of a time): a period of time 기간

Don't hold on to anger, hurt, or pain.
They steal your energy and keep you from LOVE.

- Leo Buscaglia

EXERCISE
종합 연습문제

다음 문장이나 구절들을 될 수 있는 대로 빠른 속도로 읽어보라.

1   Hot air / accompanied by high relative humidity / feels warmer than it actually is.

2   He saw a familiar face / he couldn't put a name to.

3   Four years passed / with Barbara's prayer unanswered.

4   An increase in a nation's money supply, without an accompanying increase in economic activity, will tend to result in higher prices.

 구문

"without an accompanying increase in economic activity"
= unless (it is) accompanied by increase in economic activity

5   One may have a great deal of information about a language without being able to use the language at all.

6   When all is summed up, a man never speaks of himself without loss; his accusations of himself are always believed; his praises never.

7   There is no way / she could have found it in her heart / to murder anyone.

8   It is a myth / that a preposition is a word / you should not end a sentence with.

9 Perhaps being Jewish is not something / you can remove like a change of clothing.

10 Conrad Junior had died, and his father had refused to accept it as the accident it had been.

11 Children are not stupid. They recognize insincere praise as the manipulative "buttering up" (that) it is.

12 A particular kind of bamboo / with tough, hollow stems / a foot thick / reaches heights / of 120 feet.

13 The room opened onto a veranda / with steps / leading to a small garden / surrounded by a high wall.

14 An acid is a chemical compound / with a sour or bitter taste / that usually unites with a base / to form a salt.

15 Cement is a grey powder / made from limestone and clay / which is mixed with sand and water / in order to make concrete or mortar.

16 The simplest act / an atom can do / is to move. The next simplest act is to join with other atoms / to form molecules. Just about all atoms can join with others / to form molecules of one sort or another.

17 She smiled at Scarlett, a smile / of such genuine good will / that Scarlett felt warmed by it.

18 The most heinous offense / a scientist as a scientist can commit / is to declare / to be true / that which is not so.

 구문

"that which is not so" = "what is not true"

19 The child is endowed with unknown powers, which can

guide us to a radiant future. If what we really want is a new world, then education must take / as its aim / the development of these hidden possibilities.

20 Indeed, philosophers and logicians since the days of Bacon have been entirely clear on this point: deduction makes explicit / information that is already there. It is not a procedure by which new information can be brought into being.

21 I lost track of time / as field succeeded endless field, then looked at my watch / with a startle.

다음 두 번역 중 어느 것이 합리적인지 생각해 보라.

(A) 들판이 끝없이 이어져 있었기 때문에 / 나는 시간 가는 줄을 몰랐고 / 깜짝 놀라서 / 시계를 보았다.

(B) 나는 시간이 얼마나 흘렀는지 몰랐는데, / 들판이 끝없이 이어져 있었기 때문이었다. 그러다가 나는 내 손목시계를 보고 / 깜짝 놀랐다.

22 Of all the characteristics of ordinary human nature, envy is the most unfortunate; the envious person wishes to inflict misfortune and does so whenever he can with impunity; but he is also rendered unhappy by envy.

밑줄 친 부분에 대한 번역으로 어느 것이 합리적인지 결정하라.

(A) 자기는 해를 입지 않고 / 남을 불행하게 할 수 있을 때는 언제나 / 그렇게 한다.

(B) 언제든지 가능하면 그렇게 하면서 / 자기는 벌을 받지 않는다.

23 He claims she is too controlling and manipulative, the same qualities (that) she despises in him.

24 People usually feel insulted when a young person, and a stranger at that, calls them by their first names.

25 Lady Oxenford appeared unperturbed, but Lord Oxenford kept clearing his throat noisily, a sure sign of tension.

 구문

"a sure sign of tension"

= "a sure sign that he was tense(=perturbed)"

26 A three-foot rise in sea levels (one possibility for sometime in the next century) would submerge a quarter of a million miles of the world's coastlines.

27 The priest was in his seventies, with an outward frailty / that belied his inner strength.

28 Children may, and justifiably so, interpret criticism as simply another form of punishment. Such negative feelings block productive behavior.

29 Besides being poisonous to breathe, ozone has a bad effect on farms; according to the Environmental Protection Agency, the ozone in America's air cuts crop yields by about 12%, / a cash loss to farmers and customers of more than $2 billion a year.

30 The criticized infant, said the famed psychotherapist Harry Stack Sullivan, develops a generalized feeling of "bad-me." The preschooler / with destructively critical parents / may become / what Sullivan called "malevolent child" / — one who tends to protect his self-image by seeking out and finding only the negative aspects in other people, even if they are gentle and helpful.

31 Traveling on a bus, I overheard a small boy asking his father numerous questions, all of which were answered by, "I don't know, son." Undaunted, the child persisted, with the same result. Finally he asked, "Dad, do you mind me asking you all these questions?"

   "Not at all, son," came the reply. "It's the only way to learn."

32 One afternoon, I was in the backyard hanging the laundry when an old, tired-looking dog wandered into the yard. I could tell from his collar and well-fed belly that he had a home. But when I walked into the house, he followed me,

sauntered down the hall and fell asleep in a corner. An hour later, he went to the door, and I let him out. The next day he was back. He resumed his position in the hallway and slept for an hour. This continued for several weeks. Curious, I pinned a note to his collar: "Every afternoon your dog comes to my house for a nap."

The next day he arrived with a different note pinned to his collar: "He lives in a home with ten children — he's trying to catch up on his sleep."

He who has made up his mind will never say IMPOSSIBLE.

- Napoleon

Slowly I began to understand that
when I was depressed or angry at a particular circumstance,
It was because I HAD CHOSEN to adopt that attitude.
In other words, I made the choice.
I believe that we each enact our own personal dramas in life
according to what we want to experience.

- Shirley Maclaine